KT-439-573

Mentor development for teacher training

A scenario-based approach

University of Hertfordshire School of Education
Edited by Dr Anne Punter

UNIVERSITY OF HERTFORDSHIRE PRESS

First published in Great Britain in 2007 by
University of Hertfordshire Press
Learning and Information Services
University of Hertfordshire
College Lane
Hatfield
Hertfordshire AL10 9AB

The right of Anne Punter to be identified as editor of this work has been asserted by her in accordance with the Copyright, Designs and Patents Act 1988.

© Copyright collection 2007 Anne Punter

All rights reserved. Copyright in individual chapters belongs to their respective authors and no part of this book may be reproduced or utilised in any form or by any means, electronic or mechanical, including photocopying, recording or by any information storage and retrieval system, without permission in writing from the publishers.

British Library Cataloguing in Publication Data
A catalogue record for this book is available from the British Library

ISBN 978-1-905313-15-0

Design by Geoff Green Book Design, CB4 5RA
Cover design by John Robertshaw, AL5 2JB
Printed in Great Britain by Antony Rowe Ltd, SN14 6LH

HAVERING SIXTH FORM
COLLEGE LIBRARY

WITHDRAWN FROM HAVERING COLLEGES
SIXTH FORM LIBRARY

Mentor development for teacher training

A scenario-based approach

Contents

Preface
Anne Punter

It has been my pleasure to draw together and to edit the material for this book, in order to provide a dynamic resource for the development of teachers as mentors. The book is particularly aimed at more experienced mentors who are ready to grapple with and advise on how to resolve the issues and problems generated by initial teacher trainees in schools. When a trainee is strong and capable, the mentor's role is an easy one; it is much less so when a trainee needs extra support for reasons such as those captured in the thirty-four scenarios in this book.

The rationale for this book is twofold. First it is, of course, to help mentors to support trainees more effectively. As a teacher trainer responsible for trainees' experiences on school placement, I am constantly engaging with how to support mentors in schools in being able to share their expertise more effectively. Mentors who are encouraged to be clearly analytical about the process of mentoring will be able to address trainees' needs in a structured way and also will be able, consciously, to draw on their own rich bank of professional skills. These scenarios are based on real-life teacher-trainee issues. Experienced mentors will be able to relate to many of the scenarios and may even remember a trainee they worked with who exemplified the persona in the scenario. The scenarios are designed to stimulate an analytical and problem-solving approach to the issues faced by the trainee and the mentor. There is no single 'right' answer to dealing with multi-faceted problems, but the material prompts an in-depth identification of what the issues are and a consideration of how to manage the complex set of factors towards a resolution.

The scenarios are grouped into three stages, the first having a very structured set of questions and prompts. Stages two and three offer less scaffolded direction on how to process the material and allow mentors with greater experience to work with more autonomy. In this way the text offers differentiated support and progression. The text can be used by mentors individually, or for school/Initial Teacher Training (ITT) provider group mentor development sessions.

Qualified Teacher Status (QTS) Standards are referred to generically throughout the text because we all recognise professional qualities and practices, across time and across the regularly revised versions of the teaching Standards. I am to become intimately acquainted with the third set of QTS Standards to be published during my time in teacher training. Although they have a different set of reference numbers from the previous iterations, I have no doubt that they capture those professional qualities and practices that we would all agree are essential for gaining QTS.

The second reason for producing this text is to offer material that provides a stimulus for mentors to demonstrate and to develop further the skills and expertise, as evidence for their own career advancement. We must all recognise and celebrate the immense value of good mentoring: it is often the key factor in determining whether or not a trainee meets the QTS Standards. Training providers cram into lectures and seminars as many theories, concepts, applications and practical examples as time allows, but the make or break training experience is in school, where trainees really discover how to teach, what are their strengths and what are the areas of practice they need to develop. A mentor is the critical friend who makes that journey with the trainee, who adjusts targets and expectations to suit that specific person in that particular school context, who mops up the tears if something in school or at home has gone badly and who says "Well done" when a hurdle has been crossed. It is totally appropriate that, at last, professional bodies – the Training Development Agency (TDA) and the General Teaching Council (GTC) – have documented *Standards* and *Core Dimensions* that can be met by teachers carrying out a mentoring role and that these *Standards* and *Core Dimensions* form part of a differentiated and progressive scale of teacher competences. Teachers now operate in a professional context where, from newly qualified status (NQT) up through the career steps to headship (NPQH), there is a need to identify and articulate what we are doing as professionals and how we are doing it; the demonstrable development of skills and expertise is central to career progression in an evidence-based profession. This text provides an analytical, problem-solving and reflective approach to mentoring, and its use as a training manual can form part of a mentor development programme that is certificated and linked to the TDA Eastern Region and GTC criteria. The material is specifically linked to the Mentor Levels designed by the TDA Eastern Region Steering Committee, of which I have been a member.

The scenarios for the book were originally written by members of the School of Education, University of Hertfordshire, drawn from their extensive experience of the issues arising from trainees on school placement in primary and secondary schools: Adenike Akinbode, Rosemary Allen, Peter Bloomfield, Julie Bowtell, Dr Helen Burchell, John Burden, Barry Costas, Sally Graham, Dr Bridget Hoad, Dr Joy Jarvis, Phil Lenten, Dr Roger Levy, Anne Mansey, Alex Mercer, Mandy Phillips, Dr Anne Punter, Bernice Rawlings, Mary Rees, Prue Ruback, Dr Kit Thomas, Carol Timson, Val Warren, Marian Woolhouse. The guidance prompts on how the scenarios could be used and Chapter 5 on the theoretical underpinning of mentoring strategies were written by Dr Bridget Hoad. Bridget has also played a major part in crafting the book.

The School of Education, University of Hertfordshire, is pleased to acknowledge the Training Development Agency grant for this project.

Dr Anne Punter
School of Education
De Havilland Campus
University of Hertfordshire
Hatfield, AL10 9AB
Email: a.l.punter@herts.ac.uk

Introduction
Bridget Hoad

Welcome to this active approach to mentoring trainees who are following one of the initial teacher training programmes.[1] The unique relationship between trainee and mentor in school-based learning is to be recognised and valued. Through participating in the everyday school-based lives of trainees, the mentor comes to new understanding of classroom practice and mutual learning occurs. The distinct roles of the trainee and the mentor are negotiated and re-negotiated as confidence and competence increase. This selection of scenarios mirrors the lived experiences of trainees and mentors, their dilemmas and reflections.

The scenarios may be used by one person working independently, by pairs, working with a facilitator or in small groups where the foci may be shared. They may be used by mentors and colleagues in school-based settings or in university partnership settings. Mentors may feel there is a place to use them to challenge more 'expert' trainees.

All scenarios are intended to give sufficient information to foster decision making. However, in some scenarios the detail has been left open to interpretation deliberately. Those working with the scenario should impose their own reality on the situation, for example giving the Year group the trainee is working with or the subject specialism.

The diversity of organisation and nomenclature of mentoring within schools is recognised. The trainee in the secondary phase is likely to experience a network of subject mentors led by a professional mentor. In

---

[1]   PGCE Post Graduate Certificate in Education, secondary, and primary, full-time and flexible routes, GRTP Graduate and Registered Training Programme
BA with QTS
BEd

early years and primary phases the mentor may be the class teacher or an appointed mentor (training co-ordinator) from within the school. The contact between the mentor and university tutor will differ according to which programme the trainee is following. The scenarios seek to reflect this diversity in practice. Further explanation of the differing roles is to be found in Chapter 5.

Each scenario is linked explicitly to the Training Development Agency (TDA) Eastern Region Mentor Levels 1–3 Descriptors and Performance Criteria (Appendix 1). Whilst references to the current Standards for attaining Qualified Teacher Status (QTS) are not made explicitly, it is expected that mentors will be familiar with these and bring these to the discussions associated with the tasks.

Aims

This portfolio of scenarios and associated tasks aims to promote the mutual professional development of mentors and trainees. It has as its first goal the enhanced effectiveness of mentoring in schools, which in turn will impact upon effective practice in school-based training. Its second goal is to support the mentors in sharing and developing good practice with colleagues within and beyond their school setting.

Objectives

The objectives are:

- To examine what constitutes an effective teacher;
- To recognise the beliefs, values and attitudes that mentors bring to school-based training;
- To develop effective mentoring skills grounded in good practice;
- To demonstrate and disseminate effective mentoring skills for colleagues, including moderating trainees;
- To promote practice of and evaluation of mentoring strategies for continuing professional mentor development;
- To use outcomes to plan for the improvement of staff performance in mentoring.

Chapter 1

Working with the scenarios
Bridget Hoad

Rationale

Scenarios are plausible situations designed to challenge assumptions and stereotypes. They stimulate reflections on issues and dilemmas within an interactive problem-solving approach. As dynamic situations they reflect the relationship between trainee and mentor and serve both as an analytic and synthetic tool.

The scenarios presented here include skills-based, problem-based, issues-based and speculative-based scenarios (Errington, 2003, p.11). Scenario 16 illustrates a skills-based scenario as the mentor demonstrates management skills which Rosie the trainee finds hard to emulate. Scenario 13 gives an example of a problem-based scenario as Sam's opportunities to develop are gradually closed down by the teacher mentor. Jo and her mentor in scenario 6 depict an issues-based scenario, where the mentor questions whether Jo should be allowed to continue as a trainee. Scenario 14 has many characters and we are asked to empathise with each, speculate what they may be experiencing and how they might be feeling, then make proposals to move the key character, Simon, forward.

The structure of the book

Following this introduction the scenarios are presented with accompanying activities. The scenarios within each stage may be used in any order. There is a progression within the activities.[2] Stage 1 scenarios involve mentors working within a given support structure. Stage 2 scenarios require mentors to work independently within a support structure, whilst Stage 3 scenarios give opportunity for more advanced mentors to work independently, possibly with the support of a facilitator.

Following Stage 1 scenarios (numbers 1–10) a selection of strategies is offered which mentors will discuss. This will lead to a proposed strategic response to the issues identified. The scenario then continues to offer the rationale for an appropriate response. Activities following Stage 2 scenarios (numbers 11–20) ask the mentors to identify the key issues and offer strategic responses before considering some suggested responses. The two sets of responses are then compared and evaluated. Mentors arrive at their own response to the scenario in light of the discussion. The scenarios in Stage 3 (numbers 21–34) reflect the complexity of many trainee and mentor experiences. Activities following these promote questioning and consideration of other possibilities, a reflexivity that goes beyond the depicted scenario.

Appendix 1 contains the TDA Eastern Region Mentor Levels 1–3 Descriptors and Performance Criteria. The scenario exercises in the book provide opportunities for mentors to meet these performance criteria at each of the three, hierarchical levels and so be able to produce evidence of professional development, to be submitted at performance review or at other similar career assessment points.

A theoretical background to the craft of mentoring follows the scenarios, in Chapter 5. Appendix 2 contains a reading list for those interested in exploring further the theoretical underpinning of mentoring.

Learning through scenarios

The scenarios and activities are designed to stimulate reflections on the role of mentor both as practitioner and adviser, in the classroom, in the school and beyond. They aim to challenge assumptions and stereotypes. There is no single 'right' solution to the issues and dilemmas but the opportunity to voice and explore many possible responses. Scenarios allow negative as well as positive outcomes to be confronted. They provide opportunity to prepare for and rehearse what to do in the face of the unexpected, contemplating the possible consequences of the responses.

Scenarios are used to learn from others and with others to find new

2   (see p. 13) Stage 1 and 2 scenarios are linked to TDA Eastern Region Mentor Levels 1–2 Descriptors and Performance Criteria. Stage 2 and 3 scenarios are linked to TDA Eastern Region Mentor Levels 2–3 Descriptors and Performance Criteria. (Additional information is given in the scenarios.)

solutions to recurrent problems. Through discussion we can see events from another person's viewpoint and take the opportunity to explain alternative views; to explore competing stories. Social and cultural factors which may not be apparent may be exposed and situations reconstructed in light of new understanding.

Identities of mentor and trainee are fashioned through their inter-relationships and professional experiences within and by the setting in which they find themselves. The importance of the meetings between mentor and trainee – and university tutor – is indicated in all scenarios. The process of communication is paramount. In using scenarios collaboratively with other mentors there is opportunity to develop questioning in non-threatening and non-confrontational ways. Through discourse surrounding the scenarios, mentors become skilled at identifying the strengths of trainees and come to understand the best ways to promote their development.

The model scenario in this chapter exemplifies the approach you might take to working with scenarios whether individually or as a member of a group.

As you read the scenarios:

- **Identify the issues** as you see them;
- **Prioritise** those issues and be ready to **justify** your decision, **acknowledging any constraints** as you see them;
- **Expose your interpretations** of the scenario and **explore alternative interpretations;**
- **Interrogate any assumptions** that you have made;
- **Propose strategic responses** to the issues you have prioritised and, where possible, **assign a timescale** in which to achieve your goals;
- **Contemplate the outcomes** and possible consequences of your proposals.

Facilitating groups working with scenarios

Advanced mentors are encouraged to facilitate mentor training beyond their own schools.[3] Whilst the scenarios may be used by individuals, the value of discursive interactions with colleagues cannot be underestimated and individuals are encouraged to share with others, for example, in online

3   TDA Eastern Region Mentor Level 3 Descriptors and Performance Criteria

conferencing. Facilitating group work likewise should be focused on the value of interpretation, discussion and tentative solutions to problems.

The practical considerations of optimum group size, group dynamics and shared experiences should not be ignored. As with the mentor-trainee learning conversations, mentor-mentor learning conversations should be held in a setting conducive to co-participation. Time allowed for discussion should be agreed and, following discussion, the steps towards problem solving should be encapsulated and recorded for whole group review.

The facilitator's role should be impartial and not seek to influence the outcomes of the scenarios. To this end good observational and listening skills are essential as the facilitator selects the salient information from the discourse. The facilitator should be ready to give renewed direction to those who may have lost sight of the goal, but should avoid introducing new ideas which are not owned by the group. This renewed direction may arise from sensitive challenge. Where there is potential conflict between group participants this too should be managed to steer the group to potential solutions to the problems which have been identified. These potential solutions may be shared with others through re-presenting the scenario.

Particular attention should be given to the group's analysis of socially constructed and cultural issues. Here, co-participants may strive to be politically correct or to reflect current thinking but in so doing may avoid confronting real issues. Under-represented groups within the teaching profession, such as those with declared disability,[4] may not find a voice within the groups.

Scenarios lend themselves to creativity. Whilst those presented here are in narrative, scenarios may be dramatised, used as decision board games, storyboards or flowcharts. They may be approached through analysis and hypothesis generation which act as a catalyst for dialogue between the participants. The very action of engaging with the scenario is self-perpetuating, as in the act of engagement a new scenario unfolds. The facilitator should capture this potential learning for further professional development.

---

4   TDA data collated November 2004 shows four per cent of those recruited declared a disability (source: DATE, Disabled Access into Teacher Education)

A model for working with scenarios:

Learning outcomes

In working with this scenario you will:

- Identify the key issues where the trainee may need support;
- Make explicit any assumptions you hold as practitioners;
- Identify and discuss a range of possible strategic responses to the key issues;
- Evaluate and prioritise possible strategic responses to the identified key issues.

Working with the scenario

Read the following scenario. You are going to interpret the scenario from the differing perspectives of those involved.

Consider first the mentor's position as the class teacher, then as the mentor to the trainee and finally as a partner with the university tutor.

Next consider the scenario from the viewpoint of the trainee being observed.

What can be said about the children's learning experience?

Enthusiastic, didactic Steve
The context of the scenario

The trainee is beginning his third week on his first assessed block placement. The school is well resourced and the class teacher is friendly, supportive and an experienced mentor. He has encouraged the trainee to reflect on his practice both verbally and in writing. The mentor is concerned by the trainee's apparent **inability to reflect**. What is more the trainee seems **unable to appreciate the *value* of critical reflection**. In the trainee's opinion his practice is good but the children themselves lack motivation and intelligence to learn. He models his own teaching on a favourite teacher he had when he was at school. This leads to a consistently **didactic** teaching style. He appears enthusiastic about science and this is his main strength.

The scenario from the mentor's observation report

The lesson is planned outlining clear phases and there is some attention to resources. The learning objectives are vague and the links between them and the teaching and learning activities are tenuous.

Steve opens dynamically with a question and answer revision phase. The questions, although closed, are well planned, gain the children's attention and elicit the responses he expects from them.

The second phase is a rather didactic explanation of his key points, supported by clearly labelled diagrams on the board. After fifteen minutes the children are becoming restless and distractible. Steve continues to talk to them enthusiastically.

In the next phase Steve directs the children to a written activity which involves copying diagrams and definitions from a textbook. He has not explained this clearly and the children rely heavily on the support assistant for further explanation. Steve responds to those with their hands up, but does not stop the class to explain further and help overcome the difficulties they are facing.

The final phase of the lesson is a brief plenary and the children leave in a well-ordered manner.

Immediately after the lesson, Steve's evaluation was that his class management was sound, his subject knowledge was very good and he communicated this well to his pupils.

Identify key issues within the scenario. Remember you are free to choose the age of pupils, the phase in which Steve works or the subject he teaches. (You may wish to extend the activity by considering whether the changes you make lead to the identification of different issues or strategies.)

Key issues within the scenario

- Learning outcomes are vague.
- Activities are not matched to children's abilities.
- Control and power are vested in Steve, not the children.
- Steve is concerned with written outcomes.
- Steve is concerned with content knowledge – surface learning.

Discuss and list any assumptions that you make in drawing inferences or conclusions. For example, you may assume that the trainee has been co-operative or perhaps less than co-operative! We may assume that the mentor is happy to take on the role; on the other hand there may be issues surrounding the way he was selected for this trainee.

Assumptions

Because of Steve's didactic teaching style he has not yet formed a truly representative idea of the children's levels of ability, hence there is no drive for differentiation. Learning outcomes are vague. *We assume that Steve has had instruction in devising outcomes and that the mentor's role is to hone the necessary skills. Alternatively, he may be relying on the mentor for supplementary instruction because his understanding at this point is unclear.*

Steve's enthusiasm for his subject and emulation of his favourite teacher contrive to support his didactic style. He believes as he learned successfully in this way, therefore his pupils should. If they found difficulty it was due to their own lack of motivation or 'intelligence to learn'. *We assume Steve has had the opportunity to get to know the pupils and has received information from the class teacher about the differing levels of achievement within the group. Alternatively, Steve may be working with an age group with whom he is uncomfortable.*

In pursuing a didactic style he is maximising his control over what he presents as learning and avoiding taking risks. *We assume that this is due to the stage of development within the course and that with further experience Steve will feel more ready to hand some control to the pupils. Alternatively, he may not have observed the mentor modelling self-regulating approaches.*

His concern for written outcomes owes much to his own experiences of learning. *We assume that Steve values written outcomes as evidence that pupils have been engaged in learning, and this boosts his identity as an effective teacher. Alternatively, Steve may not have received encouragement in using other assessment strategies.*

Steve is concerned with content knowledge – surface learning. *We assume that Steve's didactic approach stretches across areas of the curriculum or other taught subjects. Alternatively, his familiarity and confidence in science may have led him to 'deliver' his subject knowledge. In areas where he is less confident this may be less prominent.*

Possible strategic responses

Below are some possible responses the mentor might suggest. Read them through and discuss the merits of each to arrive at an evaluation.

Consider whether there are alternative potentially effective responses which should be included.

Prioritise the responses and justify the group decision.

1.

- The mentor opens the dialogue with a positive response to Steve's obvious enthusiasm for the subject. He focuses attention on the **learning outcomes**.
- He establishes why Steve selected these learning outcomes.
- He invites Steve to explain the short plenary session. Can Steve suggest ways in which the learning outcomes, main activity and plenary might be linked to give him more information about his focus pupils?
- The mentor takes one child as an example and works through his or her experience of the lesson in relation to Steve's learning outcomes. Is there evidence that these have been achieved and if not what adjustments should be made to make the learning objectives more focused?
- He asks Steve to share any individual formative assessment he has following this lesson. Together they work on learning outcomes for the next related lesson with an action plan for Steve to complete the subsequent plan independently.
- The mentor continues to monitor constructively.

2.

- The mentor invites Steve to reflect on the positive outcomes of the lesson.
- The mentor begins with a resumé of the introductory phase of the lesson which was more successful. He leads him back to the fifteen minutes of didactic explanation and what he observed in the children.
- Together they tease out possible reasons for the observed behaviours in this phase of the lesson.
- The mentor suggests **interactive activities** that may involve the children in this phase of the lesson.
- Steve agrees to incorporate at least one such approach in the planning for the subsequent lesson, to implement and evaluate the interactive strategy.

3.

- The mentor congratulates Steve on the well-ordered manner in which the pupils left the room, a good foundation for **empowering** the pupils.
- He focuses Steve's attention to the written activity and asks him to consider the **role of the support assistant**.
- The mentor focuses Steve's reflections on the demand for attention at this phase of the lesson and suggests reasons for this.
- The mentor summarises the issue of matching tasks to the abilities of the children, beginning with one or two. How might the planning be **differentiated** to ensure that all pupils have the opportunity to demonstrate their understanding whilst being appropriately challenged?
- Steve agrees to identify two children on the subsequent lesson plan whose work will be differentiated in one way.

Now that the group has evaluated the possible responses to Steve's professional practice agree the course of action following this lesson observation. Make a plan for Steve's progression including a realistic timescale.

Evaluation

This is Steve's first block placement. He is building on what he believes is a successful teaching style and is forming his own identity as a teacher. In this case the mentor brings practical and theoretical experience to the situation and is also mindful of the need to meet the QTS Standards.

The pupils are on the whole compliant in their learning but with appropriate targets Steve should develop a more participatory approach to teaching and learning.

Chapter 2

Stage 1 scenarios
Members of the School of Education Staff

Introduction

1. Read through the scenario and identify what you see as the key issues. Remember you are free to negotiate change of the phase, age group or subject area.
   (The issues may be positive or negative but the aim is always to propose ways to move the trainee on.)

2. Prioritise those issues and be ready to justify your decision, acknowledging any constraints as you see them.
   (For example, a trainee might have weak subject knowledge, and short-term pertinent targets related to the current topic may be appropriate over the duration of the placement. A different issue might be foregrounded whilst this issue remains in the background.)

3. Share your initial thoughts with others if working in a group. Whether you are working individually or in a group expose your interpretations of the scenario and explore alternative interpretations.
   (You may believe the trainee is not well prepared because s/he does not devote sufficient time, whereas another mentor might believe the lack of preparation is due to poor explanation of what is required, and yet another may see this as lack of understanding which needs to be addressed through modelling.)

4. Interrogate any assumptions you have made.
   (A trainee in a second practice on a three-year course may have received

good reports from the first practice but the opportunities offered may have been restricted or the expectations may have been lower than those in the second setting.)

5. Read through the strategic responses offered following the scenario. Locate what you see as the key issues (1 above) and consider what you believe to be the most appropriate response.
   (Question: what are the skills the trainee should develop and what are the skills the mentor will rely upon? You may feel that your issues are not identified or the strategic responses are not what you would choose. Make your case with the support of the responses offered.)

6. Contemplate the outcomes and possible consequences of your proposals.
   (For example, you may have set targets with the trainee with a review date. How do you respond if the trainee appears to ignore these? The trainee might have progressed beyond the classroom to extra-curricular activities which are overseen by another member of staff. How do you assess progress in this area?)

7. Evaluate what you have learned from engaging with the scenario.

8. Take the mentor's role and assess the level achieved against the TDA Eastern Region Mentor Levels 1–3 Descriptors and Performance Criteria (Appendix 1).

Scenario 1

Avoid 'treading on anyone's toes'

Ethan is a PGCE trainee in his final primary placement. He has gained most of his educational experience in the private sector. He says that he believes pupils in the private sector are motivated and parents are supportive. He has not found it easy working in mainstream schools but has impressed the staff by his efforts to get to know the pupils and families. He has done this chiefly through the extra-curricular activities.

Ethan's lesson plans are detailed and include differentiation. He communicates his expectations to the teaching assistants who adopt his clear planning with ease. He prepares potentially stimulating resources with the use of excellent ICT skills but does not allow the pupils to exploit these fully.

During the tutor's second visit to observe Ethan teaching, the mentor tells the tutor that it has not been easy to build a relationship with Ethan. In the post-observation meeting with the tutor, Ethan says that the pupils rarely meet his learning objectives. In his opinion they are not motivated to learn and do not question. He believes this is a part of the classroom culture and it is not his role to change this. He justifies this by saying that he is a visitor in the school and has less experience than those already working there, so he should avoid 'treading on anyone's toes'.

Ethan's entrenched views that pupils in the private sector are more motivated militate against him reflecting on ways of engaging pupils. His planning becomes increasingly curriculum-driven and assessments of learning increasingly negative.

Possible strategic responses

1. The learning outcome for Ethan is to set realistic learning objectives

- In a meeting between the mentor, the trainee and the tutor, give praise for the **detailed planning and excellent use of ICT** and acknowledge the trainee's contribution to **extra-curricular activities**.
- The focus turns to the **learning objectives** of the lesson. They invite the trainee to give his opinion as to whether he believes these were achieved.
- Jointly they reflect upon **the interim steps** to achieving the learning

outcomes. Did the trainee consider the pupils' abilities and make these interim steps explicit for the pupils?
- The mentor suggests they **collaboratively plan** the follow-up session using the trainee's ICT skills to produce stimulating resources and the mentor's and teaching assistants' skills to engage the pupils.
- Mentor and trainee will **jointly evaluate** the lesson and **set targets** for the following lesson.[5]

2. The learning outcome for Ethan is to explore the value of interactive strategies and set targets for their inclusion in planning

- The tutor and mentor, meeting with the trainee, praise the way he **communicates** his learning **intentions to the teaching assistants** and receives feedback.
- The tutor and mentor discuss the view that the trainee is a visitor with relatively less power within the school and suggest ways **to interact constructively with the staff team**.
- The tutor may explore the relationship between the trainee and the mentor, the mentor and the trainee. What opportunities can be created to **share views** on the pupils' approach to learning?
- The mentor suggests **alternative strategies** which will encourage pupil questioning, discussion and acceptance of others' viewpoints. Ethan is offered the opportunity to observe another teacher. He sets himself a target to include one strategy in the next lesson, to evaluate it and review.[6]

3. The learning outcome for Ethan is to create an environment which facilitates formative assessment

- The tutor and mentor discuss with the trainee what he has learned about the **school culture** through his involvement in extra-curricular activities. How is this borne out in his own classroom?
- Together they look at the **physical environment** of the classroom and analyse ways the trainee and pupils may have more open access to each other.

---

5 TDA Performance Criteria for mentors: towards level 1, 2, 3:
  - a willingness to engage in professional dialogue with trainees
  - provide a model of effective classroom support in planning
6 TDA Performance Criteria for mentors: towards level 1, 2, 3:
  - liaise with colleagues to support trainees' pedagogical knowledge

- They encourage Ethan to reflect upon the **knowledge base expectations** he holds. Compare this with the reality of the situation and suggest ways the trainee may assess understanding through **formative assessment** and open questioning.
- They encourage the trainee to acknowledge the need to **work from the pupils' achievements, their skills and knowledge**.
- They set targets to include skills such as **formulating questions** within the future lessons. They **monitor** progress towards engaging pupils and promoting questioning opportunities.

Scenario 1 continued

The tutor acknowledged the mentor's feelings that the relationship between her and Ethan had not been easy. In speaking with Ethan it appeared he felt that the relationship with the mentor was what he expected from a school placement. He was confident in his own abilities but framed the rare meeting of learning objectives in terms of the pupils' inadequate subject knowledge. The tutor focused attention on the clear planning and excellent preparation of resources. She asked Ethan how he felt when the work he had prepared had not been fully exploited. Initially he appeared unconcerned, but then backtracked to show his genuine disappointment. The tutor was able to suggest small steps that Ethan might take to introduce interactive strategies in his lessons (2). Once these were in place, Ethan would be able to use the interactive strategies for drawing out formative assessment (3). With formative assessment in place Ethan would be able to know the pupils' achievements better and plan incremental steps towards the larger aim (1).

What have you learned from working with this scenario? Continue the list:

- Trainees may find the classroom setting more challenging than is apparent.
- Mentors may define their own success by the success or otherwise of their mentees.
- Trainees may plan exhaustively but may need to observe the mentor in practice to gain the skills of implementing the plan.

Scenario 2

Working effectively with adults

Mary is nearing the end of her final school placement. She is a mature trainee who in her previous career held senior management positions. Lesson observations by both the mentor and the university tutor indicate that Mary is an excellent teacher in terms of planning, subject knowledge, class management and structuring effective learning. The reports from her first placement indicated that she showed promise and was well organised.

Following the final observation visit by the university tutor, the mentor has asked to speak with him. In considering the final report and reference he has "grave concerns about Mary's professional values and practice". He explains that staff have felt Mary is "often very bossy" in her dealings with them and has limited skills for working as part of a team. He adds that she does not express appreciation of the work of her colleagues; she prefers to do things for herself rather than with others. She tends to 'manage people' rather than work collegiately. These views have not been shared with Mary so she is unaware of these perceptions of her.

Possible strategic responses

1. The learning outcome for Mary is to develop reciprocal team work

- In the post-observation meeting with Mary and the mentor the university tutor asks Mary to **reflect** upon her achievements both within the class and within the school.
- The tutor asks Mary to describe how she has worked with other staff members within the school. Are there some areas where she has been more successful than others and can she suggest ways **team work** could be developed further?
- The tutor builds on Mary's **perceptions** of her role as a team worker and puts the alternative views of the school staff to open discussion on perceptions and the way behaviours may be construed by others.
- The tutor suggests an activity which could be **planned jointly** and implemented before the end of the placement. This suggestion will be shared with the mentor/professional mentor to allow for evaluation.

2. The learning outcome for Mary is to reflect upon and use transferable skills

- In the post-observation meeting with Mary the tutor and mentor comment positively on the **rigour of the planning**. They direct Mary's attention to the QTS Standards. In order to provide an evidence base the mentor asks Mary to write a few paragraphs on the ways in which she feels she is **meeting her professional role in working with colleagues**.
- Mary is asked to visit a trainee in another school. She should draw up a checklist which she could use in observation or interview. The checklist would show what she is looking for as evidence of **effective team work**.

3. The learning outcome for the mentor is to be objective in recognising success

- The tutor discusses with the mentor what the school has already done to encourage Mary in **effective team work**.
- The tutor gives the mentor opportunity to express her own concerns and works towards ensuring that she knows her role is valued.
- Mary asks the mentor to **model** team work through **collaborative planning** including herself and the teaching assistant(s).
- The mentor asks Mary to include in her lesson plan an **evaluation of the roles of the adults**.

Scenario 2 continued

The mentor had intervened because of pressure from staff. The inclusion of the trainee in meetings had led to a destabilising of routine and long-serving teachers were threatened by the confidence of the trainee. The mentor, aware that the intervention had come late, qualified his report to the tutor praising Mary for her organisational skills.

The tutor and mentor met to discuss what had led to the build-up of concern about Mary (3) and Mary was asked to include the evaluations of adult roles in her plans as a means of countering the subjective comments of 'bossiness'. Strategy 2 would provide Mary the opportunity to hone her skills outside the present setting. There was no previous report of weak team work so Mary should be encouraged to move on rather than account for her present situation. She has the potential to be a good senior manager but in this setting has not fully appreciated the masked politics of the school. The fact that this has been brought to attention at a late stage indicates some weakness in the managerial qualities of the team. To encourage professional development of the mentor and colleagues they might be asked to suggest how they would approach encouraging Mary to improve team work (1). Reflection on their own role in this would help them to see the extent of the perceived problem.

What have you learned from working with this scenario? Continue the list:

- Issues should be dealt with in a non-confrontational way as they arise.
- Each of us brings experiences and expertise to the learning situation and this must be positively recognised.
- It is not always easy to cast ourselves in the role of learner.

Scenario 3

Maintaining control

Chris is more than halfway into his first term as a Graduate Trainee. His planning file indicates that he is well organised and gives thought to preparation of appropriate resources. He has been observed working with small groups and appears to have a good relationship with the pupils.

The tutor and mentor jointly observe a literacy session which is well structured in his plan. He launches into a tightly controlled whole class introduction. The pupils are receptive and participate eagerly.

At the transition time Chris sets one task which is to be completed by the pupils working in their established groups. This necessitates their moving from the existing seating arrangement and collecting exercise books and resources. Noise breaks out and there is a haphazard claiming of books and resources. Pupils begin to shout above one another and Chris's response is to quell the class by shouting.

The initial response to Chris's raised voice is to go about collecting material with less noise. Chris continues to reinforce this by making threats which the pupils appear to ignore. They settle noisily into their groups and work through the task with mixed application. There are many interruptions, some of them unnecessary, and Chris is occupied responding to individual pockets of disruption.

The time for break arrives before Chris has the opportunity to prepare for the plenary. The pupils draw his attention to the break time and he disperses them. As they leave in a somewhat disorderly way, Chris flashes an anxious glance towards the tutor and mentor.

Possible strategic responses

1. The learning outcome for Chris is to manage transition times

- Prior to talking with the trainee, the tutor and mentor review previous observation notes and professional training plans. Have there been any references to **class management** in the past, particularly in dealing with transitions? Has the trainee been aware of this area of professional development and if so is it a focus area?

- In the post-observation discussion the tutor and mentor invite the trainee to give **his perception** of the whole session.
- The tutor and mentor share with the trainee observations on the literacy session and together they discuss alternative strategies, particularly for **transition points** in a whole class session, e.g. how materials and resources might be distributed; which self-checking strategy might Chris use before launching into threats; how he might deal with unnecessary interruptions which deflect him from his intended course and take time away from the plenary.
- **Targets** for implementing the agreed strategies are set and a **review** date agreed.

2. The learning outcome for Chris is to reflect on the mentor's strategies for handling transitions and choose to implement one which is suited to his teaching style

- In the post-observation meeting tutor and mentor **identify the positive progress** in the first part of the lesson. They ask the trainee to suggest why this part of the lesson was successful.
- They establish the trainee's strength in planning and preparing appropriate resources. With the trainee they **identify the critical point** in the lesson where he was not able to implement his planning.
- Together they **analyse the events** that led up to the disruption and suggest alternative approaches that Chris may have seen modelled.
- They suggest planning should include detail specific to **management of transitions** until such time as the trainee and pupils become confident with the routine and expectations.
- The mentor reiterates the **value of including the plenary** for both the pupils' learning and the teacher's assessments.

3. The learning outcome for Chris is to become confident in establishing behavioural expectations of the pupils

- In the post-observation meeting mentor and tutor ask for the trainee's views on the whole session.
- They focus on the **structure of the session** emphasising the positive points in the planning and introduction.
- They ask the trainee about the group activity and whether there were alternative ways of **establishing expectations** of the pupils in this part of the session. They suggest strategies that might be useful.

- The tutor enlists the support of the mentor in providing a **management structure for transitions with this particular group**.
- The tutor suggests the trainee takes time to **observe his mentor** in similar transitions, with a focus on time management.
- The mentor suggests Chris should explore **the behaviour, sanctions and rewards policy** of the school so that he is supported in his control of the class.

Scenario 3 continued

Chris felt that he was not coping with the situation and that this was not something that would come with practice. He felt he needed explicit instruction in how to regain and maintain attention and motivation. He was able to take the pupils' view that the lesson was not sufficiently engaging but did not see this as the first concern. The first part of the session had gone well. Perhaps he was trying to do too much too soon? He would observe the mentor at transition times (2 and 3) with a renewed focus. Whilst he had had opportunities to observe he had not at that stage appreciated how important transition times were in terms of management and organisation.

The mentor agreed to this but first outlined the key organisational points. Chris was encouraged to revisit the behaviour, rewards and sanctions policy before observing (3). The mentor and Chris would then discuss why certain approaches were used and preferred to others. They would explore how to deal with the unexpected by using the support of the policy.

Once Chris had more opportunity to observe the transitions he would be in a better position to work out his own strategies and evaluate them (1). The mentor appreciated Chris's concern to be seen as 'a teacher', but also knew that Chris would need these practical experiences to translate his plans into actions.

What have you learned from working with this scenario? Continue the list:

- Trainees may need explicit instruction supported by demonstration and modelling.

- Procedures an experienced teacher takes for granted are often difficult to articulate for trainees. Modelling followed by trainee questioning in an open climate is often an effective teaching tool.
- Mentors' skills include those of judging when to intervene and when to let events run their course so that trainees can learn from the experience.

Scenario 4

'They play in the afternoon'

Iain is a PGCE trainee in the fourth week of his final placement. Early Years is his chosen phase and he is in a Reception class.

The tutor has visited twice in the mornings and has observed a communications, language and literacy (CLL) session and a mathematical development (MD) session. Each one of these was adequately planned, with specific learning objectives and activities relevant to the age and aptitude of the children. The CLL session was particularly well planned and covered some of the National Curriculum level 1 literacy objectives. The mentor recorded positive feedback in her own observations and Iain evaluated the session realistically.

A third visit took place during the afternoon session beginning at 1:30pm. The tutor looked through the file for a plan but was unable to find one. The timetable stated 'activities' for the afternoon. When the tutor asked Iain for the plan for the intended observation, he looked very unconcerned and said, "They play in the afternoons and I use this time to catch up on my planning." Looking around the room, the tutor could see that the children were engaged in a variety of tasks which linked to a zoo visit the class had made the previous week. The tutor circulated around the activities, whilst Iain sat and did his paperwork. Iain occasionally looked up from his paperwork to check the children were on task.

Possible strategic responses

1. The learning outcome for Iain is to develop his understanding of how young children learn

- The tutor asks Iain to clarify his rationale for the session observed and to identify what individual children have learnt.
- The tutor asks Iain to articulate the principles of how children learn through play. Together they look at the principles underpinning Early Years education. They are set out and explained fully in the Curriculum Guidance for the Foundation Stage (CGFS) (QCA/DfES 2000 pages 11 to 17).

2. The learning outcome for Iain is to understand the role of the teacher in supporting children's learning

- The tutor explores with Iain a range of strategies to support and extend child led learning through play (questioning, active listening, developing constructive relationships).
- The mentor arranges for Iain to observe other practitioners working in the Reception class. He is asked to reflect on the following questions:

  - How do practitioners support child initiated play?
  - How do they ensure that the children feel safe, valued and included?
  - How do they establish a purposeful and stimulating learning environment?
  - How do they provide a balance between adult-led and child-initiated play?

3. The learning outcome for Iain is to understand the importance of assessment in the learning and teaching cycle

- The tutor arranges with the mentor that Iain should have an opportunity to observe one child engaged in both adult-led and child-initiated play.
- Using these observations as a starting point, the mentor engages in a professional dialogue with Iain to begin to plan possible next steps for this child's development and learning. Reference is made at this stage to the CGFS through selecting the most appropriate Stepping Stones (SSs) and Early Learning Goals (ELGs) that he decides the child has met.
- Together with the mentor, Iain identifies two next learning steps for the child and clarifies his role in supporting the child. These next steps could be planned as either child-led or adult-initiated play opportunities in indoor, outdoor and out-of-setting contexts.
- The mentor models planning an afternoon session which takes account of her knowledge, from her observations and assessments, of all the childrens' learning in the class. Iain observes this session being carried out and makes observations of the children ready to plan the next day's session.
- The mentor arranges for the tutor to observe Iain leading a child-led play session that he has planned for.

What if?

The mentor lacked experience of planning and supporting child-initiated play and preferred to provide adult-led activities?

What have you learned from working with this scenario? Continue the list:

- Trainees may appear to be confident and it is easy to avoid confrontation, but all trainees can be stretched further in their professional development.
- With skilful mentoring trainees may be drawn beyond their comfort zones and this sometimes involves the co-operation of colleagues, which in itself offers training possibilities.
- Appearances can be deceptive; a mentor who is concerned with the trainee's professional development will probe to gain insights into what should happen next.
- Trainees may not intend to deceive but may not know what there is to be learned. Mentors hold the overview.

Scenario 5

'Recording assessment – why?'

Sally is in her second term of the Graduate Teacher Programme. She performs very strongly academically, and has shown herself to be competent from the start. Her subject knowledge, planning, teaching and classroom management are all very strong. Her planning file is detailed and kept up to date and she reflectively evaluates her teaching. Her assessment file has not yet been seen.

The mentor asked Sally for her assessment file. She had explained that this was not in school because it was too heavy to carry. The mentor reiterated the requirements of the assessment file and the need for collating evidence. He asked her to make sure it was up to date and to bring it into school the following day. She was also asked to have it with her in school for the following planned tutor visit.

Sally brought the file as asked. On looking through, the mentor found little evidence of assessment. The evidence that was there was too general and not linked to the learning outcomes. Comments such as "Mark enjoyed this lesson", "Sophie did well" were repeated frequently. When the mentor asked Sally about the obvious gaps in the assessment file she revealed that she did not see the value of completing assessment records. The mentor shared this with the tutor on the next visit.

Possible strategic responses

1. The learning outcome for Sally is to track the assessment of two pupils against the planned learning outcomes

- In the post-observation meeting, the mentor and tutor return to the lesson planning and **targets for the focus pupils.** How will Sally assess whether these pupils have met the intended learning outcomes? Where will this be recorded? How will Sally plan for their future development?
- The mentor models for Sally the **links between planning, learning outcomes, assessment and future planning.**
- He models how this may be **tracked through planning and assessment records** and used for reporting progress.

2. The learning outcome for Sally is collaboratively to set targets for two pupils

- Together with Sally the mentor investigates where **target setting** may be found in the literacy framework and use this as a working model. They **assess** where two focus pupils are at present and what would be expected of them within the next few weeks. They set targets which can be shared with the pupils and monitored by them with help from the teacher.
- The mentor explains the **school's target setting policy**. How does this relate to the class and to individuals?
- The mentor sets the task of meeting target setting requirements for the focus pupils. This may be done in **collaboration** and structured to meet the school's requirements.

3. The learning outcome for Sally is to gather a record of pupils' work to show progression and demonstrate a variety of assessment strategies

- In the post-observation meeting the mentor **praises the positive achievements** of the lesson just observed. He asks about the learning of two focus pupils identified on the lesson plan. What are their achievements at the end of this session?
- He asks Sally for her assessment of these focus children. What is her **evidence** and how can she set this up robustly? What alternative methods could she use both to gather evidence and to record it?
- He checks that Sally understands and appreciates the **purposes of assessment.**
- The mentor continues to **monitor the trainee's assessment file** including assessments on lesson plan evaluations.

Scenario 5 continued

Sally's strengths in other areas of learning encourage the mentor. He checks that Sally has had some academic grounding in assessment. In recognition of the fact that he wants Sally to see assessment as part of a seamless planning cycle, he is reluctant to ask her to complete records retrospectively. At the same time he does not want this to lapse and become habitual. Sally has expressed a lack of interest in assessment, possibly because she has viewed this as an additional workload.

The mentor realises that he will need to capture her imagination to motivate her. He returns to her obvious elation when she has completed a successful teaching session. "How do you capture that to sustain the feeling?" Sally says she goes back to look at the work and she remembers the anecdotal comments the pupils have made as they worked, the way they seek reassurance or suggest ways to develop what they have done. The mentor asks if she can recall her responses and the mental notes she makes to herself for the future.

Gradually Sally begins to see the picture building up and she offers to gather a portfolio of work from two pupils she remembers particularly clearly. She could write captions to accompany the work and suggest what she might expect them to do next (3). The mentor says that he would like to see them and together they could set some targets for which the pupils will be responsible (2). Once she has caught up with this, she should include two focus pupils for assessment in each of her plans (1). This could be through records of work, narratives or checklists. They would look at alternatives a little later.

What have you learned from working with this scenario? Continue the list:

- Sometimes the distance to travel seems too great so we do not set out. When the distance is broken down, then we feel we could have done it anyway! The mentor has to judge the attitudes and disposition of each trainee and recognise when the goal is too distant.
- Each of us has our own style, our likes and dislikes. The mentor has to find the least daunting way to achieve the necessary goal.
- A focus upon a perceived problem can sometimes cloud the positive achievements.

Scenario 6

Valuing diversity or reinforcing barriers to communication?

Jo is a mature Graduate Trainee halfway through her first term of training. She speaks English with a strong Jamaican accent. She appears organised and creates a purposeful learning environment. The pupils in her class enjoy a positive working relationship with her. The staff at the school report that she has fitted in well and that she has also become involved in extra-curricular activities.

Jo's planning does not reflect her apparent organised approach to classroom teaching. It is scruffy and includes minimal detail but is beginning to address the essential areas of aims and learning outcomes.

The mentor has expressed her concerns to the tutor also saying that Jo's subject knowledge appears to be weak. Jo's written accuracy is a worry for the mentor. She explains that Jo has made several spelling errors on the whiteboard and when marking pupils' work. The mentor questions whether she has the essential skills to continue teaching.

Possible strategic responses

1. The learning outcome for the mentor is to use skills of diplomacy to discover Jo's awareness of the apparent problem

- In discussion with Jo the mentor finds out if she is **aware of her apparent difficulty** with written accuracy. Can she **identify the impact** this might have on the effectiveness of her teaching?
- She checks whether Jo has **disclosed a disability** such as dyslexia. Is she already receiving support with written work? (Disability Discrimination Act.)
- The tutor suggests that Jo should be encouraged to attend a **voice and communication workshop** at university which will help her to focus on her spoken clarity, which in turn will help her grammar and spelling.

2. The learning outcome for Jo is to devise and implement strategies to help in grammar and spelling

- The tutor arranges a **joint observation** of a literacy lesson with the mentor.
- Together they discuss any areas of joint concern and how these may be addressed.
- They meet with Jo and identify the apparent difficulties with spelling, suggesting a **range of strategies** which may help her in both grammar and spelling.
- Jo selects one or two strategies to be implemented and observed during the following week.
- In the regular meeting with the mentor, together they **evaluate the effectiveness of the strategies in helping the trainee to achieve her learning outcomes.** Is more support needed?

3. The learning outcome for Jo is to identify one particular theme within the subject to be taught and research this to increase her confidence level

- In discussion with the mentor, they identify the specific concerns with regard to **subject knowledge.**
- Together they identify ways the school might support the student through **use of existing resources and/or ICT.**
- The mentor agrees that she will meet with the trainee at least once a week. The trainee will prepare draft plans and the mentor will direct her to **resources** which will support her subject knowledge.
- The mentor will **make time available** at the end of each day to ensure the trainee has prepared in terms of **subject knowledge** for the following day.
- The mentor and tutor will carry out an observation which will **focus on subject knowledge.** In the evaluation they will ask the trainee to verbalise how she will increasingly encourage the pupils to take responsibility for developing their subject knowledge, including homework as appropriate.

Scenario 6 continued

Jo felt that she had a good relationship with her pupils. She felt she could share with them the difficulty that was apparent to others but not to herself when writing. She agreed to undertake a screening for dyslexia. Whilst Jo had never felt she was dyslexic, she was willing to accept that strategies used to support pupils with dyslexia could be useful for her. Her difficulty remained that she could not recognise when she was in error.

The mentor recognised the potential Jo had in her relationships with the pupils. Her concern that Jo should not remain in teaching was based more on protection (1) than a belief that Jo was not suited to the profession. Once Jo had shown willingness to disclose her apparent difficulties to staff and pupils, the mentor determined to support her (2). She was prepared to spend extra time with Jo to check spellings and provide aides-memoire.

Balancing this need for attention against encouraging Jo's autonomy was not easy. She could not wait for Jo to come to her because Jo would not see the need, yet she did not wish to appear overbearing. The nature of the relationship took on new dimensions and soon the mentor was able to move attention towards Jo's subject knowledge (3).

What have you learned from working with this scenario? Continue the list:

- The mentor's role is dynamic and both mentor and trainee are changed by the experience.
- The mentor used the partnership with the university tutor to express her concerns, but did not feel able to talk with the trainee about them. Sometimes a third party will help to look for a solution where none seems apparent. The perceived status of each character within this triad had a role to play.

Scenario 7

Being flexible or being robbed of opportunities to move on?

Kerry is a PGCE trainee. Favourable reports from her previous school placement focused on her well-structured planning, her disciplined approach to assessment, her willingness to work with colleagues and her understanding of individual needs. Her work with pupils who had English as an additional language was particularly commended in her last school. Kerry felt positive as she embarked on her final placement.

In her induction meeting the professional mentor familiarised herself with Kerry's records. She commented that Kerry would not find any pupils for whom English was an additional language in the school, but intimated that her experience in working well with colleagues would be useful to her. The professional mentor was then unexpectedly called away, leaving Kerry to find her way to the classroom where she met the supply teacher. She did not meet with her subject mentor before the placement began, but other staff members did their best to provide her with the necessary planning and policies. Kerry was resourceful and prepared herself well.

When the tutor visited to observe Kerry, she found that she was making good progress and the pupils were responding well to her. The professional mentor praised Kerry for her confidence and competent approach to whole class management and expressed great satisfaction with her achievements. Kerry, meeting with the tutor, disclosed that she had some concerns about the way the placement was going. Whilst she had been given a timetable and had agreed which lessons she would be teaching, on three occasions these planned sessions had been disrupted. Some pupils had been withdrawn without prior notice on one occasion, the timetable had been changed unexpectedly to facilitate a pre-arranged visit on a second occasion, and resources which had been booked were suddenly required by a different group on the third occasion. Kerry felt her flexibility was being taken advantage of and support she would have welcomed for her professional development was not forthcoming.

Possible strategic responses

1. The learning outcome for the personnel jointly is to identify career development paths for Kerry

- The professional mentor arranges a meeting between the subject mentor, trainee and tutor to **assess progress and identify developmental paths**.
- Together they explore ways that the trainee could **extend her experience** and present areas of expertise within the school.
- They identify any **external training opportunities** that Kerry could participate in and disseminate to/with other staff members.
- The professional mentor focuses on one area of interest that the trainee would particularly like to develop and **sets targets**.
- **Progress** towards the targets is **reviewed** and included in the final reference.

2. The learning outcome for the subject mentor is to involve Kerry in reflexive practices

- The subject mentor **reflects** with the trainee, emphasising the good progress she is making.
- She asks the trainee to take time to write down what she feels she needs to do in order to **continue her professional development**.
- The subject mentor and trainee **evaluate** what has been written. What steps can the trainee realistically take towards these goals and what support can the mentors offer? Are there any constraints which could be reduced or overcome?
- The mentors invite the trainee to **work with colleagues** on an internal staff development project which utilises her strengths and areas of interest.
- Both agree a **regular and discreet time for monitoring** and evaluating progress in wider school activities, **setting new targets**.

3. The learning outcome for Kerry is to be proactive in seeking professional guidance from the subject and professional mentors

- The tutor gives the trainee an opportunity to **say how she is feeling** when plans are disrupted. She encourages the trainee to share this with the subject mentor, offering to mediate as necessary.

- The tutor encourages the trainee **to identify why these events might occur** and what could be done to minimise any disruption.
- The tutor invites the trainee to suggest what she might do in future if she found herself in a similar situation.
- The tutor leads the trainee in **reflection** on the reasons why she feels she is not being supported in her professional development and what action she should take to address this.
- Together they discuss the **strengths** the trainee has. They **identify** a potential area where she might work with colleagues to share resources and/or expertise, then they approach the mentors.

Scenario 7 continued

Kerry, though disgruntled initially, thrived on the additional impetus of involvement in the internal staff development project (2). She was welcomed by other staff, and their views on her contributions were fed back to the professional mentor. The subject mentor reported that it was unusual for a trainee to be involved at this level, believing that it was expecting too much of trainees who already have a full workload (1). Kerry, however, welcomed the opportunity and intended to use this as valuable experience in her job interviews. For all Kerry's enthusiasm for the additional involvement she had not used the interpersonal skills (3) necessary to achieve this for herself. This proactive approach remained an area for personal development.

What have you learned from working with this scenario? Continue the list:

- Trainees deserve support at all stages of their practice, just as mentors do.
- Communication in the school appeared to be lacking and Kerry for one reason or another did not seem to have access to a communication network.
- Induction programmes must be comprehensive enough to allow the trainee to function beyond the ability to find the classroom!

Scenario 8

Determined to succeed

Ayisha is about to embark on her second assessed placement. In the interview when she applied for the course she seemed very quiet and passive. When challenged about this she showed enough positive force of character to be offered a place on the course.

Her first placement was not a resounding success but the school made some adaptations to accommodate her. She was not able to manage the classes as expected. The school, concerned about the pupils' learning, contacted the university to say that Ayisha's class contact had been reduced. The tutor visited and observed Ayisha teaching. She did not present herself confidently – she appeared diffident and found it difficult to command attention with her voice. The tutor suggested two or three changes that she might try to make to boost her self-confidence, then asked the mentor to monitor her progress up until the next scheduled visit.

The mentor rang before the agreed time and said that although there had been some progress since the class responsibility was reduced, there were misgivings as to whether teaching was the right career choice for Ayisha. The tutor in her final visit discussed this further with the mentor. They were able to record some progress toward confidence building and Ayisha herself was determined to continue upon her chosen career path.

The second assessed placement will be in an equally challenging school. Ayisha is making pre-placement visits and she reports that the staff are very supportive. She feels confident about her subject knowledge and planning skills but is concerned about what "might go wrong when I am with the class alone".

Possible strategic responses

1. The learning outcome for the mentor in the second placement is to prepare and set realistic targets for Ayisha, devising an effective induction strategy

- The tutor asks Ayisha to ensure that her **records are made available** to the mentor and staff with whom she will be working.

- The tutor encourages Ayisha to **identify her strengths** to the mentor and note where she lacks confidence. The tutor asks that Ayisha may be supported contingently to make the transition from team teaching to whole class responsibility. **Reiterate the expectations of the trainee in order to meet the Standards.**
- As a triad, they **set realistic targets** for the duration of the placement with regular review dates.

2. The learning outcome for Ayisha is to prepare proactively for the practice based on her self-assessment

- The tutor and mentor at the initial meeting in the placement will discuss with the trainee what she sees as her **strengths** and any barriers to progress.
- The trainee is asked by the tutor to **devise an action plan** based on the information that the school has given her, so that she is adequately prepared for meeting the teaching obligations.
- The tutor and mentor meet with the trainee and present some **scenarios** to her. They ask for verbal responses to the events or issues within the scenarios. They structure their questioning to help her **analyse the skills** she will need in order to respond in the way she proposes and **devise a checklist** that she may use herself to prepare her to meet likely challenges.
- The tutor suggests that Ayisha should **research opportunities for assertiveness training** and/or attend voice and communication workshops in the university.

3. The learning outcome for Ayisha is to identify transferable skills

- With the trainee, the tutor or mentor examines the **motives for choosing teaching as a career.**
- Together they **assess Ayisha's progress towards the goal** of becoming qualified to teach. Is the course meeting expectations?
- Ayisha identifies professional development since the beginning of the course. Are there **skills which are transferable** to other careers?
- The tutor arranges for Ayisha **to visit a school in a different phase,** asking her to focus particularly on management strategies she observes. Would a change of phase be appropriate?
- Together they set **a time target** by which the trainee will be making progress in her second placement or will have given these options due consideration.

Scenario 8 continued

The mentor met with Ayisha and was impressed by the way she led the conversation. She was assured that Ayisha was well motivated to achieve the course. Ayisha for her part contributed well to setting targets and welcomed the structure of the review dates (1). Whilst the mentor was pleased at the initial progress, she had reservations about Ayisha's dependency. Once Ayisha had begun to settle in, the mentor would review Ayisha's action plan (2). The mentor anticipated that she might have to lead Ayisha for some time, but in fact the preparation was beneficial and Ayisha soon became more assertive (2). Towards the end of the practice she was able to plan how she would use her experiences to approach course-based tasks (3).

What have you learned from working with this scenario? Continue the list:

- Ayisha may have been 'waiting in the wings' before flourishing. The mentor's sensitive approach and preparation were worthwhile, but at what cost to herself or the school?
- Ayisha's first placement experience was not happy, yet she had the fortitude to use this experience to prepare the way for the second placement. Acknowledging and facing up to failure are important for mentor and trainee.
- Ayisha's motivation for continuing the career path is unquestionable. Is Ayisha's self-image one of an effective teacher? Was this image shared with the previous mentor or were they working with different images?

Scenario 9

I get through!

Daniel is a final year trainee with a significant hearing impairment which mildly affects his speech. He has always been diligent with his course work, meeting deadlines and achieving satisfactory results.

In this placement he has developed good relationships with the pupils who respond positively to him. He has some innovative classroom management strategies which motivate the pupils. The staff have welcomed him and give very positive accounts of his achievements.

The mentor observed a lesson which was well managed with appropriate activities and resources. The lesson plan was sketchy on detail. The observation of this lesson showed the introduction and plenary were particularly muddled and lacking in clarity. Learning objectives and outcomes were too general and could not realistically be achieved within the lesson. A review of the files showed that these were very thin although this had been drawn to Daniel's attention previously. A target had been set to upgrade the files before today; however, weekly and session plans remained inadequate.

Possible strategic responses

1. The learning outcome for Daniel is to set realistic achievable learning outcomes

- In the post-observation meeting the mentor draws out the **positive** aspects of the lesson observed.
- He asks the trainee if there are any aspects of the lesson that he felt unhappy with or not so happy. He helps him to suggest reasons why this might be so.
- He directs the trainee's attention to the **learning outcomes** and asks how he would **assess** whether the pupils had achieved these.
- Taking one example, the mentor demonstrates the breadth of the learning outcomes and how they are open to interpretation. He **models** two learning outcomes related to the focus of the lesson which might be achievable within the given timescale. **He builds on the trainee's**

strengths to ask how these might be approached as small group activities.

- He asks the trainee to suggest how the **learning outcomes** might be shared with the pupils in a way that they would understand. How might they be referred to in **the plenary** to check whether the pupils had achieved them?
- **He sets a target** of planning in detail a follow-up session which will include an introduction (key words/concepts) and a plenary.

2. The learning outcome for Daniel is to complete planning using the agreed format with attention to all sections

- In the post-observation meeting the mentor emphasises the observed **good working relationship** with the pupils. He elicits the feelings of the trainee about the introduction and the plenary phases of the lesson. **He relates the implementation difficulties to the lack of planning** and establishes whether this is a regular practice.
- In discussion with the trainee, the mentor establishes the level of training in planning that Daniel has experienced. **He reflects on what Daniel has told him** to ensure Daniel has sufficient information to **develop from medium-term to weekly and daily plans.**
- Together they **revisit the university guidelines** and proformas for completion of planning, and Daniel is asked to complete the files in accordance with the expectations by an agreed deadline. This is **monitored with short deadlines.**

3. The learning outcome for the mentor will be to model the planning and assessment strategy engaging Daniel in evaluation

- Together with the mentor the trainee will discuss the viability of the sketchy **learning outcomes**. How will learning be assessed based on these learning outcomes?
- The mentor **models** good planning including the plenary and invites the trainee to **plan jointly and team teach** the next session.
- Each selects two focus pupils for **assessment** against the learning outcomes and these will be discussed following implementation of the plan.
- Following evaluation the mentor will ask for a **verbal report** on how this information will be used in the following lesson.

Scenario 9 continued

Daniel welcomed the way the mentor modelled planning and assessment, although one demonstration was not sufficient (3). He gained a sense of belonging through the additional attention and this led him to ask more questions. When planning in future, he asked the mentor to review his plans before he carried them out. He accepted alternative ways of approaching the learning outcomes. He found that using the proformas (2) made the process more meaningful as he followed through the different stages. Previously he had been confused by the format, but now saw the reasoning behind it. In sharing his planning with the mentor he was gaining experience in writing specific learning outcomes (1).

What have you learned from working with this scenario? Continue the list:

- Daniel's hearing impairment did not affect the key issue of planning and assessment.
- He thrived following attention that he possibly felt reluctant to demand. The sense of belonging, the interdependency of neither wanting to let the other down, in the end led to more autonomy for Daniel and a sense of achievement for the mentor.

Scenario 10

Is it too much to ask?

Ben is a PGCE trainee with accountancy experience. He is large in stature with an open countenance. Ben is highly motivated to qualify and his preference is to work with pupils in the early years.

On this, his first placement, he has been keen to involve himself in school life and has enjoyed good relationships with parents. Early in the practice he asked the mentor if he may work with the whole class (of eighteen) as well as with small groups of pupils.

Ben's mentor supports him in setting realistic learning outcomes and selecting appropriate resources. He works closely with her and they set time aside daily to review and plan. The mentor regards this as a good investment of her time, believing that Ben will achieve this independently before the end of the practice.

The mentor observes Ben during a literacy session and notes that Ben's responses to the pupils show little variation. He confirms what they have to say or praises them and, following a pause, which he does not seem to know how to fill, he begins to talk about something new.

The mentor asks herself, "Is he afraid to question them in case he asks too much of them? Is he afraid they might lead him away from his intention? Does he not have the appropriate language to question at their level or is it simply that he does not know what he expects of them next?" She wondered if Ben himself was aware of what she had noticed.

Ben reaches the end of the whole group session and gives instructions for the small group work. Those working with additional adults are settled quickly, leaving Ben to circulate to ensure others are on task. He manages to achieve this as the first groups finish! He has woven in and out of small tables and chairs imploring pupils to sit, sharpened pencils, retrieved belongings borrowed by friends, inspected wobbly teeth and adjudicated over resources not shared. As he sits down with a group he looks gratefully at the adults who have managed to initiate extension activities with their groups. What would they be thinking of him?

Possible strategic responses

1. The mentor's response to planning

- The mentor will **re-assess the timescale of her expectations** that Ben should be able to identify appropriate learning outcomes and resources independently.
- Aware of the good relationship between the two, the mentor will ask Ben to give his assessment of what went well and what might be planned differently for the future.
- She will discuss with Ben the **timescales** within which he should aim to achieve each part of the session and give him **self-monitoring strategies** and include timing on lesson plans.
- In their daily meetings, having supported Ben in identifying appropriate learning outcomes, she will ask Ben to **identify challenge.** She will show him how to build this into the plan so that he begins to heighten his expectations of the pupils.
- Following discussion of the learning outcomes she will discuss how she would **differentiate** for the differing abilities within the whole group and ask Ben to take responsibility for preparing differentiated resources for one group.

2. The mentor's response to classroom organisation

- The mentor will invite Ben to **discuss his feelings** about the observed session, based on the non-verbal communication exchanged between Ben and the other adults in the class.
- She will ask Ben to **reflect on his responses to the attention-seeking behaviours** she observed. Jointly they will reconstruct the strategies that she uses as the class teacher. Together they will identify one strategy that Ben feels he might use to settle the pupils more quickly to task.
- She will suggest strategies which encourage the **pupils to manage their own resource needs** without recourse to the adult where possible.
- She will ask Ben to plan and implement a session where she is the only additional adult available to support the pupils. Ben will focus upon **giving instructions clearly** and ensuring that the pupils understand what he requires of them.
- Ben and the mentor will **evaluate** the strategies practised and the pupils' responses to them.

3. The mentor's response to questioning skills

- The mentor will discuss with Ben her observations of his **interactions with the pupils** when teaching the whole group. She will build on the receptive response of the pupils and the strength of the relationships between Ben and the pupils built up over a short time.
- She will revisit part of the observed session which she has noted in brief transcript and **suggest alternative responses to the pupils' comments.** She will model these and link the reasoning to the need for **assessment**.
- The mentor will ask Ben to consider the learning outcomes and **include questions on his lesson plan** which will support him in assessing against the learning outcomes. He will be asked to reflect as to whether these are in pupil-friendly terms and to include any vocabulary which he feels the pupils will need clarified during the session.
- Ben will include this as one of his **targets** in his professional development file and will **self-evaluate**. He will use this self-evaluation as a discussion point with his tutor, who he will ask to observe his progress in this focus area.

Scenario 10 continued

Ben's experience with young children had been limited to contact with friends' children and he was not prepared for the collective demands for attention. He valued his relationship with the mentor and was aware of the confidence she had in him. The respect he held for her professional practice allowed him to observe keenly. The mentor for her part was empathetic and did not lose sight of the potential for mutual development.

She prioritised Ben's professional development needs and gave him an overview of these (1, 2 and 3) whilst focusing first on the organisational skills (2). She would continue to support him in planning (1) but in doing this she would suggest how she would develop questioning to aid assessment (3). This oral modelling would continue until Ben was ready to take on the role of planning for which she set a target time. Meanwhile the focus would be upon organisation and giving clear instructions so that the pupils could continue the self-regulating skills she had fostered.

The tutor was impressed by the preparation and reflection which had informed Ben's self-evaluation. She was able to record progress in organisation judged against the mentor's previous literacy observation.

What have you learned from working with this scenario? Continue the list:

- The time given to Ben proved to be a positive investment, although initially demanding.
- The mentor re-assessed her expectations of Ben as he progressed at differing rates in different areas.
- A motivated trainee who feels valued will be encouraged to develop self-monitoring strategies in a supportive environment.

Chapter 3

Stage 2 scenarios
Members of the School of Education Staff

Introduction

This section contains untitled real-life scenarios. Here you are asked to identify the issues and suggest strategic responses to the scenarios yourself. When you have reached a solution to your identified problem(s) you might compare your strategic responses to those offered as suggestions following the scenario. The suggestions are not intended as definitive answers, but to act as catalysts for discussion. There is some variation in approach between them.

   You may work individually and compare your response first with that of a colleague and then with the suggestions. Alternatively you may work in small groups to arrive at your problem-solving approach, then compare this to the suggestions. In both cases you may feel that your response is more appropriate and wish to add that to the bank of possible strategic responses.

Scenario activities: Stage 2

1. What is the scenario about?
Read through, identifying whether there are any ambiguities and try to resolve these.
Assign to the scenario a title which encapsulates what you see as the critical issue(s).

2. What are the positive strategic responses to these issues?
Reflect on your proposed course of action and share this with others.
Set some SMARTER [5] targets for the trainee.

3. What are the professional skills this trainee should develop?
Identify the learning outcomes for the trainee and describe your strategic
response(s) to supporting him or her in achieving them.

4. What are the professional skills the mentor will draw on and develop in addressing
this scenario? (Refer to Appendix 1, Mentor Level 1–3 Descriptors.)
Consider the implications of your preferred strategies for the mentor and the
tutor. (Asking the question "What if...?" is often a good way to open this.)

5   SMARTER = Specific, Measurable, Achievable, Realistic, Time-related, Evaluated, Reviewed

Scenario 11

Alice

Alice has a 2:1 degree in mathematics. She has taught in the private sector for some years as an unqualified teacher of mathematics. In this role she was not required to produce lesson plans or to meet National Curriculum or National Strategies objectives.

In this, her first assessed practice, she has shown she is confident in the classroom. However, her teaching skills are limited and she needs to develop an informed methodical approach to planning and assessment.

In this practice she meets both disaffected and less able pupils and does not yet have a range of strategies to engage them. At present her behaviour management strategy is confined to raising her voice. The class becomes increasingly noisy and Alice becomes frustrated by the lack of engagement.

Alice is reluctant to accept advice from the mentor or the tutor as she believes her years of experience have taught her what she needs to know. The mentor speaks with the tutor, expressing some frustration. She feels that Alice views the Graduate Teacher Programme as a formal requirement to recognise the experience she has already gained as an unqualified teacher.

Think about and talk through the possible strategic response before reading on...

Possible strategic responses

1. The tutor's and mentor's responses to planning and assessment

- Prior to beginning the placement, the tutor and mentor check that Alice has received all necessary documentation to meet the planning and assessment requirements.
- They ensure she has a working knowledge of the National Curriculum and National Strategies requirements for the relevant year group(s).
- In the preliminary visit, they discuss the school's medium-term plans with Alice. They ask how she will translate these into weekly and daily plans.

- The mentor discusses and models how to write and evaluate a lesson plan. She refers Alice to the handbook guidance.
- The mentor sets the target of writing a detailed lesson plan for the next observation. In the post-observation meeting, the mentor asks Alice to orally evaluate the lesson and assess two focus pupils against the specified learning outcomes.
- The mentor asks the trainee to suggest how this information will be used in future planning with particular reference to the focus pupils.

2. The mentor links effective planning to behaviour management

- In the post-observation meeting, the mentor allows the trainee opportunity to talk about her experiences prior to joining the course. What did she feel was successful? Which areas did she have little experience of?
- The mentor links this discussion to the lesson just observed and identifies any strengths. She will give her perceptions of the lesson and refer to the lesson plan, suggesting this is an area for professional development.
- Together they identify areas for professional development and steps towards achieving these. They set targets which may be realistically achieved within the timescale of this practice.
- The mentor models a lesson plan for the observed lesson demonstrating how this may be made more specific. She shows that detailed preparation with appropriate activities will reduce the likelihood of difficulties in behaviour management.
- She asks the trainee to prepare an action plan, to be shared with the mentor, detailing the stages by which planning will increasingly become more specific and use previous assessments.

3. The mentor circumvents Alice's reluctance to accept advice by providing appropriate models

- The mentor asks Alice to observe experienced teachers who demonstrate a range of behaviour management strategies and write reflective notes on how these teachers operate and the pupils' responses.
- She asks Alice to reflect on a critical incident where she felt uncomfortable. What was her response and what might she do differently?

- Alice is to analyse various classroom routines establishing expectations of the pupils, identifying possible 'flashpoints' and reinforcing positive responses.

Return to the Introduction to Scenario activities: Stage 2 and check that you have addressed all four activities.

Refer to the TDA Eastern Region Mentor Level Descriptors and Performance Criteria in Appendix 1, and assess which criteria the mentor would have met.

Scenario 12

Ella

Ella is a second-year trainee who is just keeping up with the demands of the course work. She meets deadlines but always 'gets by' with the minimum of effort. Her first assessed practice was in a school with a motherly mentor. The mentor spent a lot of time with Ella during the school day and checked at the end of each day that Ella knew exactly what was expected of her the next day. She lent resources and suggested appropriate activities for the lower ability pupils. She spoke with the teaching assistants to make sure they would address any issues that might arise with the more challenging members of the class.

In Ella's second placement, the mentor has asked to speak with the tutor during the second visit. She is concerned that Ella is arriving late at school, and when she does arrive she is not adequately prepared to take the lessons she is timetabled to take. On several occasions she has begun the lesson and finished before the due time, leaving the pupils sitting or handing over to the mentor. At the end of the day when the mentor has checked that she has everything for the following day, Ella has always said that she was ready or would prepare at home and left promptly. At lunch times Ella would not join the staff in the staff room although frequently invited, nor did it appear that she was preparing in the classroom. The mentor was concerned that she could not find ways to support Ella and could not see the necessary development as the practice was progressing.

In discussion with Ella in the post-observation meeting, the tutor discovered that Ella had domestic commitments which she did not wish to be disclosed to the school staff. In her opinion she was meeting the requirements for planning but admitted her evaluations and assessment records needed updating. The pupils were responding well and she had a good relationship with the mentor.

Possible strategic responses

1. The tutor's response in the role of mediator

- In the post-observation meeting with Ella, the tutor listens to her reasons for reported lateness and leaving early. He discusses with Ella whether there are any unexplored ways around the domestic commitments. Sensitively, he points out the obligation to arrive adequately prepared and ascertains whether the existing difficulties with timekeeping are likely to be long-term difficulties.
- Together they review the records of Ella's first placement and identify her strengths. How might she build upon these in this different situation yet still show progress and development? The tutor makes clear that these targets will be shared with the mentor either by Ella or himself. The mentor will monitor progress towards the targets which Ella sets.
- He asks Ella to adjust her routine so that she leaves at the end of each day with the resources and lesson plans in place for the following day, having shared these with the mentor.
- He makes it clear that lateness without adequate explanation to the staff will alienate those who are willing to help.

2. The mentor's response to differentiation and time management

- In the post-observation meeting, the mentor elicits Ella's perception of the lesson. What were her strengths and what could she do differently to improve?
- She shares with her the perspective of the observer given the evidence provided on the lesson plan. What could be included on the lesson plan to make her intentions clear to the observer and most of all to the pupils?
- She asks Ella to include time markers in her plan to guide her and avoid rushing through stages which are important for the pupils' sound understanding.
- The mentor refers to the QTS Standards. She reiterates the value of including differentiated activities which will challenge both the least and most able.
- She urges Ella to visit the school's resource area. She models the way she considers the needs of pupils with differing abilities and asks Ella to do the same for two pupils on the following lesson plans. She invites Ella to enlist the support of the teaching assistants in helping prepare resources for individual needs.

3. The mentor reiterates expectations and requirements

- In the post-observation meeting, the mentor directs Ella's attention to the need to update the planning and assessment files.
- She talks with Ella to ensure she has the understanding of what is required and asks her to give a verbal assessment of one or two pupils across curricular areas.
- She sets timed targets by which Ella will have updated her files and shared these with the mentor and the tutor on his next visit.

Return to the Introduction to Scenario activities: Stage 2 and check that you have addressed all four activities.

Refer to the TDA Eastern Region Mentor Level Descriptors and Performance Criteria in Appendix 1, and assess which criteria the mentor would have met.

The strategies depicted here are responses to Ella's need for support, yet no one strategy is sufficient because the mentor and tutor do not have the full picture. Ella has the picture in terms of expectations. The mentor has the overview of what is to be learned. The tutor has the insight into barriers to Ella's practical experience. Suggest ways the three might work together to support Ella.

Scenario 13

Sam

The tutor's first visit to the school was at the end of the day as parents and carers were meeting to collect their children. Parents stood chatting to one another in the spring sunshine as children ran around and over flower beds, or clung to the trunks of newly planted trees. A toddler pulled at a daffodil and offered it to the carer who continued talking with her friend. She folded the daffodil in her arms as the toddler waited for acknowledgement. On that day there was optimism in the conversation between mentor, trainee and tutor.

On the second visit, prior to carrying out the observation, the tutor sensed an air of politeness, a circuitous route to the main points. The mentor reported that Sam, in her final year, was unjustifiably lacking in confidence. "She's really doing very well with my babies and they are not making it easy for her." Tutor and mentor observed Sam in a literacy lesson, which was well structured, building appropriately on previous learning and using resources imaginatively. However, space was at a premium. There were some pupils who were distracting and interrupted the planned lesson.

In the post-observation discussion with the tutor, Sam reflected well on her lesson and was quick to identify behaviour management as an area for her development:

"I am really a confident person and I know I am well prepared, but I am never left alone with the class. Even when the mentor says she has to do something, she keeps coming in to check I am all right. I wouldn't mind if she just sat getting on with her work because I know sometimes it is hard to find somewhere to go, but she keeps talking to the pupils and it undermines my confidence. When parent helpers come in she always goes over to them and tells them what to do. Last Tuesday she told me that some parents had approached her at the end of the day to say that they are not happy at the amount of non-qualified teaching contact the pupils are having. She says that she is anxious to avoid friction between the school and the parents so I am not to speak with the parents any more. She will take responsibility for receiving and dismissing them each day as if I am not here. I mean, I know she's got a point and she is supportive but sometimes I feel as if she gives with one hand and takes with the other."

Possible strategic responses

1. The tutor's and mentor's response to behaviour management

- In the post-observation meeting, the tutor asks Sam what led her to identify behaviour management as an area for development.
- Her good preparation is acknowledged by the mentor, who also seizes the opportunity to praise Sam's creative skills.
- The mentor suggests which pupils are a cause for concern with regard to behaviour management and explains their learning support needs.
- The tutor invites the mentor and Sam to suggest a creative activity which will be relevant to the planned learning and differentiated to include those pupils the mentor has identified.
- The tutor asks Sam to prepare an observation checklist whereby she might monitor the contribution of the focus pupils. As the mentor would not be present she should report back to the mentor using the checklist.

2. The mentor's response to behaviour management and working with parents

- The mentor takes the view that Sam is working hard and a few pupils are causing the difficulty Sam is experiencing.
- She cites the school's policy on rewards and sanctions with which Sam is familiar.
- She suggests some strategies about which she has learned from a recent course but has not yet implemented.
- Sam identifies one pupil whom she would like to focus upon first. She suggests to the mentor that she would like to work with the parents in reinforcing positive behaviour for this individual pupil. The mentor suggests she should act as mediator between parents and school.

3. The response to use of space in the classroom

- The mentor acknowledges that she has become accustomed to her space and welcomes fresh ideas.
- Mentor and trainee agree to trial some changes. This fresh approach leads them to consider the possible responses from the pupils.
- Both discuss the behaviour difficulties they have encountered, linking them to the pupils' need for space. Together they review their responses to unacceptable behaviours and agree a common approach where these may be due to lack of space.

Return to the Introduction to Scenario activities: Stage 2 and check that you have addressed all four activities.

Refer to the TDA Eastern Region Mentor Levels Descriptors and Performance Criteria in Appendix I and identify the areas of development the mentor will need to address on her path towards becoming an advanced mentor.

One barrier to the trainee achieving the QTS criteria in this scenario was the school's policy towards trainees' contact with parents. Suggest ways this may have been overcome.

(This scenario is included in a different format as scenario 34 in Stage 3.)

Scenario 14

Simon

Simon shares a house with two other trainees who are also working in their final placement. On Thursday night they get together and the conversation turns to their experiences in school. Simon listens as Will tells how the staff are really supportive. The pupils are sometimes challenging but usually he can manage them because he has good relationships with them. Sam says that she feels a good rapport with the pupils but is not convinced that they all give their best effort. She puts this down to the fact that the age gap between her and some of the pupils is very narrow, therefore she does not enjoy the same status in their eyes as the more experienced teachers. Simon blurts out in relief, "It's not the pupils, it's the adults that I have difficulty with."

Simon explains that his school does not share the same characteristics as their schools. He is in a large multi-cultural school which is fortunate in the number of additional adults and professionals it has employed to support the pupils:

"You would think I was lucky to have all that help, but you have to plan for them, talk with them – or at least make it clear what you want them to do – before the lesson. Then you have to make sure they feel included when you are teaching, and to top it all you have to find ways for them to report back. I know this is all very important for assessment, but they know more about the pupils than I do. They are brilliant at their jobs. I was confident at first but it all began to snowball. When it came to the planning meeting, I knew they were waiting for me to tell them what I planned, but I felt really intimidated and finished up saying nothing, so my subject mentor bailed me out."

Possible strategic responses

1. Advice Sam and Will might offer Simon

First they ask about the number of adults in the room for each lesson in order to get a picture of the point Simon is making. Is this in every lesson or in some lessons? How does he feel in lessons which have fewer adults to support in comparison to those with more support? Do the adults need to be there to support pupils with identified special educational needs or is there some flexibility in the way they might be used?

Simon is unable to answer the last question with certainty; Sam and Will suggest he **speak to the SENCO or the subject mentor to get an idea of which pupils have particular targets**.

Do any of the pupils have English as an additional language and need this support to have access to the curriculum?

Simon thinks that this is the case but all of a sudden this is getting too much for him to comprehend. How can he be expected to have such detailed knowledge of the pupils within such a short time?

Sam and Will can see his point and can see that he has to take one step at a time.

They suggest he go and see the SENCO and talk to the subject mentor. He could ask if he could use some of his non-teaching time to meet with one or two of the additional adults and find out what their individual targets are. He can make it one of his targets too.

2. The subject mentor's approach to Simon's dilemma

At a meeting with the subject teachers the subject mentor gathers all observations about Simon's approach to working with additional practitioners. She asks for illustrations from the observed practice in order to gain an overall impression of the progress Simon is making in this area. Subject teachers are invited to suggest ways they might encourage Simon. Following this assessment she arranges to meet with Simon. She emphasises the progress he has begun to make and asks him how he feels he has been getting on. Using the subject teachers' observations, she directs his attention to working with the additional practitioners and suggests this might be a useful target for future professional development.

The subject mentor arranges with the subject teachers to ensure Simon has time to meet with the additional support adults to discuss their targets for the pupils. One subject teacher, together with the support adults, meets with Simon to review and forward plan the next session Simon is to teach. Simon then attends the following planning meeting with increased confidence in the process. The subject mentor reviews Simon's progress at an agreed time.

3. How might the additional practitioners support Simon?

The additional practitioners make time to **share progress reports** with Simon at the end of each session he teaches. Where there is a need to **differentiate** work in order to include the pupils, the practitioners explain to Simon why and how this has been achieved.

Where initiating contact is constrained by time, Simon has **access to the pupils' work for assessment purposes.** A record of the session from the pupils' perspective would lend Simon insights into the need for differentiation. Any particular difficulties, for example with subject specific vocabulary, could be highlighted. This would serve as additional information for Simon's assessment file.

Where there are **resource implications**, particularly if shared resources, these are drawn to Simon's attention.

Simon makes the additional practitioners aware of his intended learning outcomes in advance of the lesson. The practitioners offer suggestions based on their experience and knowledge of the pupils **making foundations for team work**.

4. The subject mentor feels that Simon has not made sufficient progress based on the first steps taken to address his difficulties. What should happen next?

Return to the Introduction to Scenario activities: Stage 2 and check that you have addressed all four activities.

Refer to the TDA Eastern Region Mentor Level Descriptors and Performance Criteria in Appendix 1, and assess which criteria the mentors potentially meet.

Scenario 15

Henry

Henry has been moderately successful in the course. Now halfway through, he is gaining confidence and beginning to meet the QTS Standards required in terms of planning, teaching, classroom management, lesson evaluations, monitoring and assessment. The mentor reports Henry has settled quickly in the school, almost a seamless transition for the pupils, you could say. He asked about planning and schemes of work early on and observed keenly. Before he came, he had made the effort to find out about the school which the mentor found encouraging.

"We seemed to get on well from the beginning," he said. "I was more than willing to share the science planning with him because there is so little time in this placement. When I observed his first science lesson I could anticipate what he would say at the end."

The tutor has worked with Henry in a number of university-based sessions and believes that he has developed a sound, realistic understanding of the nature of schools. He has contributed to group sessions using his experiences. He is willing and positive, if a little unimaginative. The tutor senses that there is a risk Henry might be content to be a 'good enough teacher'.

Records of observations by the mentor indicated that he was very pleased with the progress Henry was making. The pupils appeared to be learning and Henry had a sound approach to teaching. The mentor noted that when Henry observed the teacher taking the class, he asked some quite perceptive questions about particular pupils and the way the teacher responded to them.

The mentor and tutor carried out a joint observation during Henry's science lesson. When they came to discuss their notes the mentor was extremely positive in commenting on what he had observed. Pupils had responded to Henry's questioning with the right answers, which indicated they had been attentive. The timing of the session had been good; in fact, they were cleared and ready for the end of the session. The tutor's notes acknowledged what Henry had achieved, whilst questioning whether there were alternative ways to achieve the teaching and learning. Could

Henry have promoted more rationalisation and problem solving through his questioning? Could he have engaged the pupils for longer and spent less time on routine procedures? The mentor's view of this was that the tutor was 'being picky' and he shared this view with Henry.

Possible strategic responses

1. The tutor's reflections during the joint observation – prior to conferring with the mentor

What shall I say to him when I see him? I need to make sure that he hears the positive comments whilst planning to move him on. I will check his professional development targets and why he chose them. Perhaps he is driven by meeting the Standards and should be more imaginative.

Maybe I should focus on the quality of the pupils' learning, noting what I see as **key episodes** in the lesson. I will take three episodes, just a few lines of teacher to pupil interchange or pupil to pupil dialogue. When I meet with Henry we can use these recorded episodes as a springboard for discussion. This might show where he wished something to be different and why. I should:

- Share my observations with the mentor;
- Identify key episodes where Henry might have developed learning opportunities for the pupils;
- Ask Henry to suggest alternative approaches using innovative resources;
- Suggest that Henry makes questioning a target for the following week;
- Ensure the mentor, who has the overview of the pupils and the school, and I are in agreement.

2. The mentor's reflections during the joint observation – prior to conferring with the tutor

He did ask me before whether I felt the more able pupils were challenged well enough, but I told him that they had achieved what he wanted from them. I believe he should consolidate his practice all round before stretching off into risk areas. I am not saying that he should not aim to include challenge – he should. I just don't think he is ready to do that yet; he has enough to do as it is. I should:

- Share my observations with the tutor;
- Share with Henry the strengths of this lesson, the detail in planning and sound links between all phases of the lesson;
- Ask Henry how he will build on the learning the pupils achieved in this lesson;
- With Henry, identify the pupils who are achieving well and suggest ways that they may be positive role models for the other pupils;
- Identify Henry's professional development target for next week – perhaps this should be giving immediate and constructive feedback.

3. The divergent views are exposed and converge

- The tutor shares with the mentor and Henry his assessment of Henry in the university sessions.
- Henry explains some of his achievements in university to the mentor.
- The mentor praises these and adds his own praise for Henry's progress in the school.
- The tutor asks Henry to identify an unexplored area of development where he might build on the practical skills he is developing.
- Henry identifies the use of additional resources to stimulate the pupils. He adds that up to this point he has felt guarded about including these as he thought the management might cause problems.
- The mentor seizes the opportunity enthusiastically, suggesting how Henry might support learning using resources he had personally customised for his lessons.
- The tutor adds that Henry should give thought as to how the resources will be presented in a way which will promote extension of the pupils' problem solving approaches. How will Henry introduce, monitor and assess as the pupils worked?
- The mentor agrees to demonstrate the inclusion of the resources and formative questioning for one group, then hand over the teaching to Henry as the resources rotate during one lesson. They will work collaboratively and evaluate at the end of the session.
- Henry welcomes the additional support of collaborative working whilst venturing into this approach.

Return to the Introduction to Scenario activities: Stage 2 and check that you have addressed all four activities.

Refer to the TDA Eastern Region Mentor Level Descriptors and Performance Criteria in Appendix 1, and assess which criteria the mentor would have met.

What steps would need to be taken if tutor and mentor maintain conflicting viewpoints?

In this scenario the mentor disagrees with the tutor and shares this with the trainee. How might this affect the professional development of the trainee and the partnership between school and university/training provider?

Scenario 16

Rosie

I suppose you could call me a late starter – Rosie, forty-five years of age. My first placement is further away from home than I anticipated but my children are teenagers now.

In all honesty I seriously considered withdrawing from the course when I first began this placement. I teach art in an all-boys school. I am finding this hard because the boys are so boisterous and I have such a quiet voice. Even when the boys are waiting to come into the classroom they are very noisy and I have difficulty making myself heard. I don't seem able to calm them down and the noise level just builds throughout the lesson. I keep looking at the clock to see how much longer I have to go, but then I think, "Well, they haven't even completed the first task yet so they won't achieve the learning outcome before the end of the lesson." The Year 7 group is particularly difficult but I do enjoy teaching Year 10. I can get around and talk with them as they work and I think I am building some good relationships with them. If only they could all be like Year 10.

What does my subject mentor say? Well, she is younger than me but she has plenty of confidence. She has noticed the difficulty I have with the boys. I did share with her how I felt when I was not in control. It worries me that the art room I normally teach in is at the entrance to the art block and is a thoroughfare for individual pupils and staff. To feel out of control in such a public arena is not good. My subject mentor basically said, "Get on with it, because we can't change it." She does not have the same difficulty, you see. A lungful of air and she has them quiet in no time, attentive and focused on the task.

Possible strategic responses

1. The subject mentor's deferential response

Well, I am new to the school and I have not had to mentor a trainee before. I got the post as head of department, which was great, but I had not realised how much time the administrative work would take. Then I was asked to mentor Rosie and thought, "Well, how difficult can it be? I have not long finished training myself so should be able to identify with her experiences."

I guess I underestimated the job. I went on the training, so I know what is expected of me. What I find difficult is pinpointing what I do to manage classes that Rosie is obviously having difficulty with. She does not use her voice well, but how can I tell her that? I suppose rather than say the wrong things I say nothing at all and that is not very helpful. Next time we talk I could ask her why she feels different about Year 10 because other members of staff report that this Year group is more difficult. Perhaps I could help her with an eye-catching display that would take people's attention as they go through the room. That way she may not think people are watching her.

2. The subject mentor's assertive response

Rosie tells me she almost left the course when she first came here. I can understand that. She does not have much confidence when she is with the pupils. Her ideas are good and she is quite creative, but what is the good of that if you are not able to inspire and motivate others?

I suppose the most important thing she has to learn is to use her voice assertively to command attention. On the other hand, if you are not naturally an assertive person that is difficult. There are no really difficult pupils in Year 10 and they are quite compliant so she probably finds those easier to manage. I have not observed her teaching that year. Perhaps she uses a different approach with them.

When Year 7 is lining up to go into the lesson there is a dreadful noise. She tries to quieten them but in the end gives up waiting and they go into the room unsettled. I do not know how she manages to teach them above the noise and the class next door must be affected too. Perhaps I ought to be there next time she teaches and use my voice to settle them. I would not want to undermine her but she really has to get this right before she can teach them. As I say, her ideas are good and she is quite creative.

3. The subject mentor's empathetic response

I will talk with Rosie today because I am sure she is not really happy. She seems to feel it is her use of voice which is the problem and I can see that this is not easy for her. But really there are other things we should be able to do to help her get around this. It must be so frustrating for her when she is working so hard. I must be sure not to appear to undermine her in any way, but I will suggest that we take a lesson together and establish some signals that the pupils must respond to. It can be presented as a drive to keep noise levels low in that part of the school. I'll ask if there is anything that Rosie would like to try that we have not yet thought of. She did come to me and made a point about the art room entrance being a thoroughfare, but we can do nothing about that for the time being. I will visit the art block at the end of school with Rosie and see if there are any physical changes we can make. We also need to raise this as an issue at the staff meeting. There might be timetabling or access issues which could be looked at to help. Meanwhile I must encourage Rosie for the effort she is making.

Commentary

All views identify the use of voice as a central issue to maintaining class management. In the first response, the subject mentor has an indirect approach and sensitivity towards Rosie's feelings. The second response uses a more direct approach of modelling the way to appear more assertive. Both approaches are potentially constructive and may be reflections of the mentor's own practices. The introduction of a display to deflect attention away from Rosie would build on existing skills, but equally may not be very successful in practice. The approach of modelling use of voice and settling the pupils is perhaps essential to future learning, but Rosie herself will need to become more assertive in order to benefit from the model. Additional classes in use of voice and assertiveness would be in order to support Rosie. Meanwhile, in the third response the mentor respects Rosie's position and suggests some team teaching. The support in this may be incrementally reduced contingent upon Rosie's increased security in classroom management.

Return to the Introduction to Scenario activities: Stage 2 and check that you have addressed all four activities.

Refer to the TDA Eastern Region Mentor Level Descriptors and Performance Criteria in Appendix 1, and assess which criteria the mentor would have met.

Rosie is clearly motivated to become a teacher. What role does the subject mentor play in this?

Scenario 17

Mark

Mark is a Graduate Trainee who has used ICT quite extensively in his former employment. However, he has had only patchy formal academic training in ICT. Nevertheless, he is hugely confident in his capabilities and subject knowledge and is very defensive should his status as a subject specialist be brought into question. He frequently bolsters this with reference to his practice before training to teach.

In addition, Mark is often explicitly or implicitly critical of the school-based ICT curriculum. He seems to feel that pupils should be made aware of what he views as shortcomings in the curriculum. He believes his experiences of 'real life' ICT have more value than teaching skills in a formal way. This leads him to take short cuts without giving the pupils explanations and they find the skills difficult to replicate. He is constantly moving on without ensuring the pupils are with him.

Mark is somewhat contemptuous of detailed lesson planning, taking the view that he has all he needs to know in his head.

At a meeting between subject mentor and professional mentor, the following conversation took place:

Subject mentor: Mark is a great asset to the school. He is extremely confident in the use of ICT and has offered to review all the public signing in the school. He is so proficient with ICT that he will get it done before the end of the practice.

I have watched him working with the pupils and they are really motivated by the practical sessions he delivers. I don't think I would be able to achieve what he manages to get the pupils to produce…but then ICT is his background. Mark just 'goes for it' *and* manages to have something to show for it at the end.

Professional mentor: I believe you have made a good assessment of Mark and his use of ICT, but I am not convinced this is necessarily good practice. I appreciate he has much experience, but I question whether his practice is not simply outcome-based. I feel if you asked the pupils to repeat one of the sequences in Mark's absence, they would have great difficulty because they have not developed the skills, simply responded to direct instruction.

Have you discussed his lesson plans for ICT with him? I have asked to see a plan, but he could only produce a very sketchy draft outline that told me nothing about how he would break the task down for the pupils. He was very defensive when I suggested that I was willing to help him.

Commentary

The issue of whether Mark is as competent at ICT as he appears is secondary to the main issue. Mark must **plan effectively** to encompass all abilities and to **demonstrate his understanding of the way pupils learn**. He teaches a range of age groups and he must show that he appreciates the differing stages of skill acquisition and understanding. It is essential that Mark reflects upon his current practice, which appears outcome-driven, and refocuses on the skills appropriate to the different year groups.

There may be several approaches to target setting with Mark whilst maintaining his confidence. The first might be to enlist Mark's skills for his own ends, recording his observations of the pupils' **preferred learning styles**, for example. Which pupils prefer to follow a written sequence of instructions, which disregard this and rely on being told? This would get Mark **to focus on the learning** rather than the outcome. Professional and subject mentors could then take him a step further and ask him to reflect on those who achieve independently and those who need support. A logical step from this would be to ask him **to plan making sure he addresses these individual differences.**

Alternatively, the subject mentor should acknowledge Mark's offer to review the signage throughout the school. She should suggest that Mark should use the time for his own professional development in order that he may 'have the edge' on other candidates when he goes for interview. She should discuss with Mark the need for planning based upon the scheme of work and medium-term plans. The subject mentor would select one class group and establish with Mark his knowledge of their individual abilities. Where Mark is uncertain she would provide her own assessment of the pupils within the group and the additional attention they might need. Together they would identify the skills necessary in order to achieve a learning outcome selected from the medium-term plan. These skills may be dispersed through more than one lesson as necessary, but Mark must identify them and show in a staged approach how he will introduce and evaluate them. The subject mentor may suggest timed episodes, ensuring all pupils are demonstrating understanding before moving on. Together they will evaluate the achievements of individuals to add to an electronic running record. The subject mentor will report back to the professional mentor who will arrange an observation with the ultimate target of demonstrating differentiated work.

Return to the Introduction to Scenario activities: Stage 2 and check that you have addressed all four activities.

Refer to the TDA Eastern Region Mentor Level Descriptors and Performance Criteria in Appendix 1, and assess which criteria the mentor would have met.

How might the subject mentor enlist the support of the university tutor?

Scenario 18

David

David has been placed in a 'high-achieving' girls' school. He has extensive knowledge, experience and love for chemistry. All his pupils show respect and co-operation and his subject mentor is very pleased with his progress.

The subject mentor and tutor make a scheduled joint observation and have divergent perceptions. Their simultaneous reflections are set out below.

The subject mentor's reflections

David has begun well and the girls are very attentive. They know they should bring their lab coats to this lesson and six of them say they have forgotten them. I think David should have reacted more forcefully to this so that it does not happen again. It shows a lowering of expectations. I shall have to ask him if he is aware of the sanctions the school uses.

He is referring back to the previous lesson and asking the pupils to recall, which is good. He ties the homework in with his intended learning for today. When he gives the homework back he seems surprised that two of them have not handed homework in on time. How did he miss this? Again this sends out a message to the girls that they can get away with not meeting deadlines.

He introduces the lesson clearly and has some really interesting resources prepared. It is a pity they have not all got their lab coats. The practical activity is going well with good regard to safety. I particularly like the way David is circulating amongst the groups and using praise for those making good progress through the activity.

He gives timed warnings for closing down the activity – good. The girls should be used to this and clear away what they have been using in an orderly manner. What will I look for in the plenary? Does he revisit the learning outcomes? How does he assess the learning that has taken place? Good, Charlotte seems to have understood. Hers is a good little working group.

The tutor's reflections

David appears well prepared with planning and resources. Are all the pupils of the same general ability because there is no evidence of differentiation on his plan? I know the school selects pupils in the top twelve per cent, but I will need to watch the differing responses to David's questions and the planned activity.

The girls are very attentive and on the whole well prepared. Some have come without their lab coats but they know where to get spare ones with minimum disruption. David does not let this interrupt him – good. He returns the homework books with liberal praise for some. What messages does this give to others? Does the praise always go to the same pupils? I will check David's assessment strategies and help him to review these from the pupils' perspective if necessary.

The practical activity is well organised and the girls respond well to his instructions. As they work he walks around the groups and listens to them, but he uses praise which simply confirms what they have done. I would like to see him go further with this. I will watch for open-ended questioning which can challenge the girls, particularly the most able. I have the feeling that their potential is appreciated but not exploited.

There are some girls who in fact are not contributing to group discussion and David is taking responses from the most voluble. How does he check that the answer given by one is understood by the rest of the group? Again there are some formative assessment issues here. It seems that the girls have been grouped in mixed abilities and there is no apparent differentiation for the lower ability, which I can now identify, having seen them working. I need to check my own assumptions here with David's help, because one girl seems to be heavily reliant on her peers. She may not be of lower ability but might have English as an additional language.

David gives a timed warning to closing the activity, which is good. The girls launch into clearing away with military precision and sit awaiting the plenary and anticipated dismissal. David summarises the activities and returns to the learning outcomes shared at the beginning of the lesson. I must ask if this is his usual pattern or whether he uses differing approaches which involve the girls on some occasions.

I must find out how well David feels he knows the individuals' abilities, how does he feel he caters for their individual needs? I should offer him strategies for open questioning and formative assessment.

Commentary

The subject mentor and tutor will need to meet prior to discussion with David and discussion with the professional mentor. They should identify the strengths that each of them has observed: the clear introduction to the lesson, interesting resources, attention to individuals and liberal use of praise. The procedural concern for bringing lab coats should be acknowledged as an expectation on the part of the pupils. David should be asked to reinforce this, but not allow it to deflect him from his main focus. Equally, he should maintain the expectations for homework. He might be supported in encouraging the girls in self-monitoring strategies so that they take the responsibility.

Attention should be turned to David's liberal use of praise and assessment strategies. The subject mentor's views on these should be sought. How reliable does she feel David's assessments are? What strategies does he employ?

Given the ethos of the school, assessment should be raised with the professional mentor as an area for professional development.

Return to the Introduction to Scenario activities: Stage 2 and check that you have addressed all four activities.

Refer to the TDA Eastern Region Mentor Level Descriptors and Performance Criteria in Appendix 1, and assess which criteria the mentor would have met.

Suggest strategies which might go towards reconciling the different viewpoints expressed.

Scenario 19

Michael

Michael is finding this third-year BEd practice more challenging than the earlier practices. This has caused him to reflect on the differences in the situations between his present and past placements. He believes the pupils he previously came into contact with were compliant and showed respect. This afforded him ample opportunity to develop his planning and assessment skills. He had known challenge in the past but had always been able to formulate some rules as the need arose. He had formed good relationships which allowed him to share humour with the pupils.

Now he felt he was struggling with class management and the behaviour of one or two pupils within a group. Instead of shared humour he was beginning to feel he was the butt of the jokes between some members of the class. They had picked up verbal and physical mannerisms Michael used without realising it and mirrored these in disrupting the class. One girl would regularly interrupt and deflect him from his course towards the learning objectives. Then some boys would add to the distraction, mimicking and introducing irrelevancies. This would escalate into verbal sexist responses. His dilemma is always that he cannot let the disruptive behaviours go unchecked, yet if he attends to them the classroom becomes a theatre complete with audience for those seeking attention.

Michael believes he has used his intuitive observational skills and knows the motivation of the pupils who distract and disrupt. He has some solutions in mind, which he shares with his mentor. Some she feels she can accept, whilst others she holds reservations about.

Michael's responses

1   Put the pupils into small groups so that the more disruptive are separated and have good working role models.
2   Remind myself to vary the way I draw the class to attention and check my nervous gestures.
3   At the first sign of interruption with the intention to waste time, I will move the pupil, asking them to change seats with an attentive pupil who is sitting close by.

4   I will move the pupil intent on distraction to the back of the class where they are not seen by the rest of the class.
5   I will seat the boys next to girls who are good role models.
6   I could carry out an activity so that pupils can identify their preferred learning styles, and then plan with that in mind.
7   I could monitor the questioning strategies I use. Do the girls have more closed questions than the boys, for instance?
8   I could make a list of my rules and expectations and display these so that I can refer to them readily.

How should the mentor respond to Michael?

Commentary

1   The success of this strategy will be constrained by the numbers in the group, the group dynamics and the space available. If Michael relies on the good role model he will need to be sure of the consistency of this model and the small group dynamics in order to avoid the disruption of the group. He will also need to consider the expectations he is placing upon the role model.
2   This in itself is a positive approach and if practised will allow him to exert more control. He must make sure, when using a variety of techniques to call the group to attention, that the pupils know his expectations.
3   This strategy has similar drawbacks to the first one. In asking the pupil to move, there is the dilemma of drawing attention to the negative behaviour. The attentive pupil may be distracted by the exchange of their neighbour and may be stigmatised by peers, so may be resentful.
4   The removal to the back of the class may be effective, but the nature of the disruption should be considered. A vocal distraction could continue or be exacerbated as the pupil continues to seek attention.
5   This strategy would be construed as gender discrimination and not recommended.
6   In principle this is an effective strategy, but one activity may give insufficient information. Michael should collect evidence to allow him to use this flexibly.
7   This strategy shows good insight on Michael's part but in order to monitor his questioning effectively he will need to enlist help from an additional adult or video recording. The fact that he has put this forward

will on its own heighten his awareness.

8   A visual reminder of the rules would avoid interrupting the flow of teaching, providing attention is drawn to them. Responsibility for compliance clearly rests with the pupils in this strategy. Michael might need to ensure the sanctions are also clear and in keeping with the school policy.

Return to the Introduction to Scenario activities: Stage 2 and check that you have addressed all four activities.

Refer to the TDA Eastern Region Mentor Level Descriptors and Performance Criteria in Appendix 1, and assess which criteria the mentor would have met.

What strategies should be in place to ensure liaison between mentor, professional mentor, and tutor?

Scenario 20

Peter

Peter had been a classroom assistant for five years before he began his training. Now in his final placement, he is coping well in an all-ability city school. He is very enthusiastic, and his drive motivates the pupils. His planning is thoughtful and rigorous, indicative of the time he invests. This planning is supported by interesting resources, which he devises with originality.

Peter uses the resources to help differentiate the planning. He also differentiates in the way that he approaches groups of differing abilities and interacts with them. His relationships with all pupils are good and he is very highly thought of by his department. The head of department has said that he would like to employ Peter on a full-time basis now, were it possible.

The mentor is very happy with Peter's progress. The targets that are agreed between the mentor and Peter are couched in terms such as 'continue to develop using ICT' and 'improve the presentation of resources'.

Below are set out two responses to Peter's achievements. The first does not include Peter in the discussions, the second ensures he has an active role.

1. Read the two alternative responses and **evaluate the effectiveness of each response for all concerned.** For example, in light of the mentor's target setting, the tutor might have been anxious to talk first with the mentor before discussing these with Peter. On the other hand, imposing targets may not be effective at this stage in Peter's professional development.

2. In reading the second response decide:

What are the necessary skills that tutor and mentor need in order to acknowledge their differing views and engage Peter?

What factors must be considered in giving feedback?

What actions should be taken when the discussion does not go as intended?

Possible strategic responses

The first response: a meeting without Peter

Three weeks into the final practice the tutor and mentor meet to discuss Peter's progress. Peter is not present to hear the conversation. He has told them he feels he is making good progress.

Mentor: I am very happy with Peter's progress. He is doing really well. Only last week Jane in the department said that he was ready to start teaching here now. We don't even have to observe him much now and he is working well on his targets.

Tutor: Yes, that's right, he has really made good progress. He manages his classes effectively, and even deals with unexpected incidents confidently. What do you think he should do next, in terms of his development?

Mentor: Well, I don't think there is much for him to work on. It is just a matter of generally getting better, tightening up, giving a bit more attention to his marking.

Tutor: His planning is thorough, with clear learning objectives which he shares effectively with the pupils. He plans for differentiation and uses a variety of assessment strategies. I was just thinking back to that assembly he did last week, 'Kick it out!', that football anti-racism project. If that is an issue being addressed by the whole school, could Peter plan to develop this or similar value-based issues?

Mentor: That is a good idea. It would give him the opportunity to look closely at organising groups to encourage pupils to work together. Or maybe he could look at cross-curricular content. It would be really useful if he could build up a bank of resources around the issue of race to use in display. I could ask him to do that as his next target – I know he will be diligent in researching the subject.

Tutor: And this could be extended in Peter's work with another class. This would be good to encourage him to address the differentiation issues in response to different learning styles. It would also heighten his awareness of group dynamics. He obviously enjoys a challenge so let's put it to him...

The alternative response: a meeting including Peter

Mentor and tutor simultaneously observe and record their observations in preparation for giving oral feedback. They discuss their observations prior to the joint oral feedback.

Peter, mentor and tutor meet in a quiet setting where they will not be interrupted. The mentor congratulates Peter and the tutor asks him to identify what made the lesson so successful. The tutor is intending that Peter should reflect on his skills and relate these to the theoretical underpinning he has become acquainted with in his reading or lectures. The mentor then asks Peter to suggest an area that he would like to develop.

Peter feels he has gone as far as he can within the targets he has agreed to date and is looking for guidance in formulating a realistic but worthwhile target. He is ambitious and would like to be practising skills which would give him an edge when seeking promotion in his employment.

The tutor suggests that Peter has made an impressive start with differentiating activities and creating resources. An extension of this would be to focus on individual learning: to analyse how he selected appropriate teaching and learning strategies, and to consider his evidence that the learning outcomes had been achieved.

The mentor asks Peter to break this down into small targets to compile an action plan.

Their joint written feedback

Key strengths:
- Good relationships with pupils – they respond well to you.
- This is a well-planned lesson which uses innovative resources. Your enthusiasm for your subject is evident.

Areas for development:
- To refine differentiation which caters for all abilities within the group.
- To link assessment strategies to the differentiated activities.

Action plan:
- Take a group of individuals that is representative of the range of achievement within the class. Create individual profiles made up of assessment data, their learning styles, their social and behavioural needs and forthcoming targets.

- Include in your planning differentiated learning objectives for these pupils which build on their identified strengths.
- Design at least one alternative method of assessment for each lesson which encourages the pupils to monitor their own progress.

Commentary

The dialogue in the first response focuses very much on Peter's achievements and his extension within the wider school setting. The suggested target would develop his skills in organising groups. He would be extended beyond meeting the QTS Standards as he applied existing skills to new situations.

In the alternative response Peter is required to reflect more specifically upon his practice, critically analysing individual achievement in more depth.

The discussion between the mentor and tutor in the first response raises questions as to whether a trainee can ever be 'left alone' with few observations. It encourages both tutor and mentor to reflect upon their own values of what constitutes 'a good teacher' beyond meeting the QTS Standards. Then both must decide the role the trainee plays in establishing the direction to take.

The alternative response strives to provide united and constructive post-observation feedback.

Reiterate:

What are the necessary skills that mentor and tutor need to discuss their differing views and engage Peter?

What factors must be considered in offering feedback?

What actions should be taken when the discussion does not go as intended?

Return to the Introduction to Scenario activities: Stage 2 and check that you have addressed all four activities.

Refer to the TDA Eastern Region Mentor Level Descriptors and Performance Criteria in Appendix 1, and assess which criteria the mentor would have met.

Chapter 4

Stage 3 scenarios
Members of the School of Education Staff

Introduction

The scenarios in this chapter offer some challenge to those critical practitioners who are deploying their mentoring skills in and beyond the classroom. It is expected that the scenarios will encourage mentors to reflect upon and challenge the effect of institutional structures. They will examine their own beliefs, assumptions and prejudices inherent in their practice and be instrumental in the professional development of trainees and colleagues. More questions will be raised than solutions found, but solutions will be proposed in the course of discussion. Resistance to alternative approaches to teaching and learning will be challenged through probing enquiry.

The scenarios take differing formats. The questions following these scenarios are deliberately less structured, and speculation is encouraged. As solutions to dilemmas are proposed, the necessary mentoring skills should be checked against the TDA Eastern Region Mentor Levels 1–3 Descriptors and Performance Criteria in Appendix 1.

It is envisaged that participants' reflections on their own experiences will prompt the writing of further scenarios which will contribute to an archive of rich experiences, of critical incidents. (See Stewart, 2003, pp.83–91 for constructing problem-based scenarios.) The critical practitioner will guide the mentor in diagnosing problems, interpreting experiences and analysing perceptions.

Scenario 21

Jane

Jane is a mature PGCE trainee with a humanities degree. For her first placement she is given a Year 4 class. In conversation with her it becomes apparent that she has a huge chip on her shoulder about what she sees as her poor educational background.

At a group meeting of fellow trainees convened by her tutor, she dominated the discussions with complaints about her class teacher. Her class teacher is also her mentor, a very able teacher and the deputy head in the school. Jane upset the mentor on the very first day in the school by criticising her teaching. She also antagonised other staff by her very aggressive manner in the staff room.

Jane's complaints rumble on as she groans about lack of time and overwork, but it is known that she has not used the time before or after school for preparation. The mentor complains that she is worn out with Jane's demands to see her after school every day. Jane complains that she should not have to wait until after school to talk to her.

The tutor arranges a meeting between herself, the mentor and Jane. When brought together with the mentor, Jane denies things she has already said to the tutor, claiming that her mentor does not allow her into the class in the mornings before school.

The mentor suggests to the tutor that whilst Jane's teaching does not show particular promise in any one area, she has the potential to achieve the targets set for her. She adds that after two weeks Jane still does not know the names of the twenty-four pupils in her Year 4 class. Her timing of lessons needs attention because she spends time talking to the pupils without backward reference to the learning objectives. She has a tendency to interrupt pupils when she asks them to feed back to the rest of the class, speaking for them.

Jane's self-assessment in the third week of her practice is that she is good at teaching but needs to improve on her subject knowledge in general.

Consider the role of the mentor. Where would you demarcate her role in this instance?

Identify points of disagreement and suggest factors which may have led up to these. How may these have been avoided?

Had Jane been a quiet non-assertive trainee and this information was elicited in a one to one conversation with the tutor, would your response have been the same?

Scenario 22

Bill

The mentor shares with the tutor her intuitive assessment of Bill. As she does so the tutor listens for evidence to support the judgements the mentor is making.

"Bill is unsure in some areas of his curriculum knowledge. He seems to spend much time on his lesson plans which are very detailed. Unfortunately, he does not think about the resources he needs and often he has not left himself enough time before the lesson to make sure these are prepared.

"I have tried to point this out to him and he appears to be listening - even jotting down notes to remind himself. Sadly it does not seem to make any difference because there is nothing in the next lesson to tell me that he has thought about what I said. I am becoming concerned because I have helped him with behaviour management strategies and I cannot see any progress in this area.

"Oh…and he has had several days' absence. He is here today because he knew you were coming, but I can predict he will have a day off this week."

As the Tutor observes Bill she reflects on what the mentor has said. The observation records seem to indicate that Bill has not been entirely successful in engaging the pupils. Where there was a lack of interactive teaching the pupils seem to have taken the lead. She wonders what strategies have been suggested to Bill? She would expect to see some evidence in Bill's reflections. The lesson is not going well.

What should happen next?

The triad of mentor, tutor and trainee are mutually supporting. Speculate on the unconscious motives of each of the participants in the scenario. How may these be reconciled in a common aim?

If this scenario had taken place in a school which was not your own, how would you, as an advanced mentor, help the mentor in this scenario to evaluate her role?

Scenario 23

George

I am subject mentor to George, a young trainee in his second placement. He is a science specialist – my own subject too – and has a Year 7 class in the science laboratory as I observe him now. I have looked at his plan and see that he does not intend to use any practical equipment this lesson. His learning objectives are clearly written, but as for the rest…I shall have to observe to see how he intends to achieve these objectives. We did discuss this lesson, but it seems as if he has changed his mind about it.

The pupils come into the room quietly and orderly, sitting ready to work. They focus their attention on George and he introduces the lesson with reference to previous sessions… That is good. I must use this as a starting point in my feedback after I have explored his perception of the lesson.

He is explaining the task he wants them to do, but perhaps I missed something. No, the pupils look equally baffled. Some are asking him to explain again, and he does so but on a one to one basis. Is he going to repeat himself thirty times? The others who do not have his attention take the opportunity to talk amongst themselves. Initially they talk to those closest to them but increasingly share their banter across the room. Is George going to do something about this? No, he is continuing to give instructions one to one but ignores those around him. Ah! He has realised and is calling for whole class attention. It takes four attempts but there is quiet now. A boy asks him to look at his work and he goes over to respond to him. Now he has lost the attention of the whole class again… missed opportunity after working so hard for it.

He has finished with that boy and now seems to realise his mistake. He tries to call the class to attention again, but peters out trying to make a deal with them all. "Just finish this, then we will…" He never gets to the end of his sentence. I notice that those who received attention early on have now finished. Others still await attention and have not yet begun. All begin to misbehave.

I assess the situation. George does not appear aware of the pupils off-task. I make the decision to circulate amongst them and intervene. All pupils were expected to achieve the same task within the same timescale

but he must know their differing abilities. Now I see that the prepared resource sheets were not circulated properly. We discussed this yesterday, and still some pupils have four and others have none.
   Where do I begin to find anything positive to say about this?

Was the subject mentor right to intervene at this point?

Whose needs were uppermost in the subject mentor's mind and why?

Walk in each of the character's shoes in turn. Explain their feelings and fears.

Explain their responses and why they reacted as they did.

How may the negative experience be used as a developmental milestone?

How should the subject mentor communicate her concerns to the tutor?

Scenario 24

Kirstie

Kirstie is a biology graduate in the latter part of her training. She has proved to be an able trainee, particularly in her subject specialism. However, in addition to teaching biology she has been required to teach physics and chemistry to some Key Stage 4 classes. These pupils are different from those to whom she teaches biology.

Kirstie has found it difficult to plan the physics lessons to the required standard. As she feels less secure in physics she relies heavily on lesson plans and schemes of work produced by other members of the physics department. Her planning and preparation are of a poor standard and the lessons she teaches appear dull. This is not commensurate with her ability to teach her own subject.

During her third week she is observed by the physics teacher who provides feedback, prior to meeting with the subject mentor. Observations of the biology lesson prove a positive experience, and Kirstie is encouraged by the comments and constructive target setting. She is praised for her subject knowledge and consistently detailed planning.

To her surprise the observation of the physics lesson receives no constructive feedback. She feels that the lesson had not gone well and anticipates that the physics teacher would be able to help her to identify ways to improve her own planning. In fact the physics teacher offers little positive comment. She implies that the 'tried and tested' lesson plan had made it easy for Kirstie.

Whilst Kirstie feels in part relieved that the physics teacher has not been negative, she feels also that she is being 'let down'. Her own assessment of her teaching in physics makes it difficult for her to accept the feedback.

The subject mentor meets with the professional mentor for discussion. The biologist is aware of the difficulties Kirstie has in planning physics and also of Kirstie's views that her efforts were dismissed by the physics teacher.

The physics teacher, subject mentor and trainee appear to hold different expectations of an effective teacher, particularly of a trainee. With reference to the QTS Standards, speculate what these might be.

In the role of the professional mentor consider the essential information you must have in order to:

- make fair and valid judgements of the trainee;
- challenge the subject mentor and subject teachers to reflect on their own values of an effective teacher. (Link the mentoring skills needed to achieve this to the TDA Eastern Region Mentor Level Descriptors and Performance Criteria in Appendix 1.)

Scenario 25

Raj

Raj is a final-year BEd trainee who is on a placement with a Year 5 class in an urban JMI School. The class is lively and contains a voluble group of boys.

Raj is intelligent and confident; a charismatic teacher with a strong grip on the class. He uses a mix of whole class teaching and small group work. However, as yet he is *not* good at organising groups of pupils. This is much to the chagrin of the class teacher, who has worked hard at encouraging pupils in discursive skills.

The school sees effective group work as one of its strengths. Raj has observed this in action but the organisation seems to elude him. He seldom differentiates work, and often activities are inadequately resourced to make the learning outcomes accessible to all. Raj thinks that he has achieved what is necessary to meet the QTS Standards and does not accept that he has a weakness in this area which needs to be addressed.

The Headteacher, who is also the mentor, has invested much staff time and training expenditure in developing group discursive skills throughout the school. After the first observation he meets with Raj and moves the discussion to what he sees as an area for Raj's professional development.

In your opinion to what extent is the Headteacher, who is also the mentor, justified in asking Raj to focus on group organisation and discursive skills? Justify your opinion.

Had the school recently invested in developing music rather than discursive skills throughout the school, and the Headteacher asked Raj to focus on this, would your response have been the same?

The Headteacher is focused on continuity and the needs of the school. As mentor, how would you reconcile the developmental needs of Raj with the needs of the school?

What are the skills Raj will learn as a result of the meeting, and how might the tutor monitor these?

Scenario 26

Nazreen

Nazreen is a Year 3 trainee on her final placement. She has a good relationship with the pupils in her classes. However, this is often at the expense of overall control of the class. She is easily drawn to respond to individual or small group distractions which divert her from the overview of the class.

The class teacher mentions to her that a group of pupils who usually work well are increasingly off-task. She says no more and Nazreen sees this as a problem with the pupils rather than questioning her own practice. Nazreen was surprised to find the class teacher step in to take control of a lesson that she was teaching.

She was angry and rang the tutor to complain about it. "There was some background noise," she said, "but no children were out of their seats." She felt undermined and humiliated. She had not been able to speak with the mentor at the school before leaving that day, but intended to complain at the earliest opportunity.

The tutor contacted the mentor at the start of school the next day and arranged a visit between all three. Role-play or visualise the mentor's alternative responses in the meeting.

The mentor has the role of meeting multiple developmental needs. Discuss what you see as the essential action points for the mentor in this scenario.

In your role as advanced mentor, explore how such an experience might contribute to in-school training and policy review.

Scenario 27

Christa

Christa is a PGCE trainee on her first placement in a primary school (Year 4) set in a large multi-cultural community. Her course work has been thoroughly researched and well presented by set deadlines. This is echoed in her first placement, where her planning is extremely detailed given the stage of the course. The class teacher, who is also her mentor, reports that Christa has asked for very little help in deciding what she should teach.

During the first visit prior to observing the trainee, the tutor, in conversation with the mentor, felt the mentor was striving for diplomacy. She was at pains to point out the strengths in planning *but...*

It appeared Christa had alienated the staff at the outset with forthright reference to her governance experience in a very different socio-economic area. The mentor felt she was trying to transfer what she had observed in one school to a very different school without regard for the essential qualities of the placement school. She questioned her unconscious reasons for wanting to teach.

After the joint observation by tutor and mentor, the tutor noted Christa's didactic style. There was a need to develop open questioning and respond more expansively to pupils' contributions. The preparation was thorough. The mentor had the benefit of knowledge of the pupils and was worried that the expectations were unrealistic given the functioning of the group. Christa was moving through her plan by providing responses when none were forthcoming. There were some pupils whom she could not call by name. The mentor wanted to see her sitting with a group of pupils but it seemed that she always kept the invisible line between herself and them.

In discussion with Christa after the observation, it was clear that she felt the lesson had gone well. Her reflections and evaluations focused on her experience of delivering the lesson, and from this viewpoint it was a job well done!

The mentor questioned whether Christa held unconscious reasons for wanting to teach. What might she have had in mind and how might this barrier be overcome?

Had the socio-economic characteristics of the school placement and the school in which the trainee gained her governance experience been reversed, how might the staff have responded?

As an advanced mentor, how would you suggest the mentor should liaise with the university tutor to promote Christa's interpersonal skills, engaging with pupils and staff?

Scenario 28

Connor

Connor has been making good progress in his PGCE course and has begun his second placement in a secondary school teaching English. He has asked to speak with the professional mentor as he feels he needs support in one aspect which the subject mentor has not been able to provide.

"I am really enjoying it here and feel I have a good relationship with the pupils. Staff are very supportive and I know I only have to ask and they will find the time for me. They have been very positive in their feedback to me and encouraged me, but there are two pupils which I have difficulty with and I can't tell what it is that I need to be doing differently. Staff just tell me to do what I have been doing as it works with most of the pupils, but these two, one in Year 7 and one in Year 8, are a bit of a puzzle. I have been told that they each have an individual education plan and I try to refer to these, but the pupils do not seem to relate the targets to their own behaviour. The SENCO tells me they are 'on the autistic spectrum' as if I should make allowances.

"What I find difficult is when everyone is busily working away and out of the blue there will be an outburst just because the seating or the displays have changed in some way. Then suddenly a boy will run out of the class and I have to decide what to do. It is all right if there is someone working with him, but that does not happen all the time. The boy in Year 8 is just as challenging but reacts differently. He will not look at me when I speak to him and his responses are really quite aggressive. The work he does never really covers what I have asked him to do, so he is difficult to assess. If I try to talk with him to help him he seems to resent the attention and answers quite rudely. Again I worry that the others will think that it will be acceptable if they behave in the same way. Perhaps they feel it is unfair that he is 'allowed to get away with it'. Am I unconsciously reinforcing the behaviours? Whichever way I look at it, I feel challenged by both pupils and should know how to react for the benefit of all the others."

The subject mentor's support was inadequate in this instance. How might the professional mentor address Connor's needs?

What strategies should the professional mentor draw upon to address the subject mentor's apparent inadequacies, e.g. training targets and Continuing Professional Development (CPD)?

Connor has taken the initiative to speak with the SENCO but the response has not helped him in practice. What role should the partnership between school and university play in supporting Connor?

Where does the subject mentor's responsibility for Connor's professional development begin and end?

Scenario 29

Alistair

Alistair is a BEd trainee in his second year working in a Year 6 class. His mentor has completed informal observations, giving oral feedback which indicates that he is meeting her expectations. However, his concern is growing as he comes to the end of the third week and he has no formal observations from her as evidence of meeting the QTS Standards. He has a good relationship with his mentor and feels he can raise the issue with her, which he does. The mentor appreciates his direct approach and assures him that the next scheduled observation will be formally recorded. She adds that she is cautious in making judgements and does want to give him every chance to succeed.

At this point Alistair raises the issue of the course-based tasks he has to complete during the placement. He apologises for not sharing these with the mentor earlier. The mentor for her part knew of the tasks but considered these as additional work to accommodate. She was preoccupied with forthcoming assessments and did not see how the tasks would meet both her purpose and the trainee's. In her view the tasks were a source of potential conflict as they were not sympathetic to her agenda. The longer she could ignore them, the less intrusive they would be. In any case, if Alistair had not told her about the tasks, then it was unreasonable of him to expect the school to accommodate him.

As an advanced mentor involved in training new mentors, identify and prioritise the issues as you see them in this scenario. Be prepared to justify to novices the priorities you set. (Check Appendix 1 for the Performance Criteria the advanced mentor will meet.)

The school values its partnership with the university. List recommendations for the school's continued role in hosting trainees.

If Alistair is to have the necessary evidence that he has met the QTS Standards, trainee and mentor must strengthen their communication. How might a third person facilitate the changes that are necessary?

The mentor does not co-operate with Alistair in accommodating the course-based tasks. What happens next?

Scenario 30

Jess

Jess had attended a departmental meeting during the pre-visit days at her placement. A trainee in her second placement, she used her previous successes in the first to assert a standing with staff in the department. She explained she had been mentored by relatively new teaching staff and took on the teaching 'from the start'. As a result of this, the subject mentor reported that she had alienated staff, who were affronted by her confidence. Jess was completely unaware of this, believing that she had a contribution to make.

In the second week the subject mentor had carried out and recorded a formal observation. Time had clearly been spent planning in preparation, but the implementation of the planning exposed large gaps in understanding. A check on the first observation made by a colleague seemed to find a similar situation.

Meeting with Jess after the second observation, the subject mentor focused on the links between the learning outcomes and the tasks set. She asked Jess to explain what she had expected the pupils to learn during the lesson. "Tell me what you want me to do and I'll do it. I'll do it. I can't stand all these questions," she said aggressively. When encouraged further she began, "I just wanted them to…"

The subject mentor sensed Jess was under pressure and took over the conversation, explaining how she might have approached the lesson. Aware that Jess was more vulnerable than she would have others know, she talked about the time she had obviously spent preparing and planning. It seemed this time was not used to its full advantage, because plans contained more detail than was evident in the implementation. Pupils were allowed to coast through parts of the lesson towards the bell. Jess was limping from learning outcomes to plenary, unaware of how to carry the pupils on the journey.

"I do work hard at planning and preparation," she said, relieved at the recognition. "I have never understood learning outcomes and need to work on implementation."

Jess has allowed colleagues a path to support her halfway through her practice. What might the professional mentor, department colleagues and subject mentor have done to make her experience different?

Had Jess continued to assert her competence in the face of difficulty what would be the role of the professional mentor?

What action might the subject mentor take to support Jess in implementing her learning objectives?

How might the professional mentor use Jess's experience to draw in new mentors?

Scenario 31

Alex

Alex is in his final year of a BEd course. He is a trainee with limited experience of managing pupils whose behaviour can be challenging.

On the first pre-visit day, the subject mentor identified two pupils whose behaviour could cause concern, but when the subject mentor was present Alex saw no evidence that this was the case. A teaching assistant had been assigned to one of the other pupils in the class. It was an agreed policy in the school that the identified pupil should be monitored 'at a distance', as it would be detrimental to her progress for her to become dependent on the teaching assistant. The second pupil identified on the day of Alex's visit was withdrawn from the class. He was a Traveller recently enrolled at the school. It was reported that he was reluctant to speak and as yet was not socially accepted by the other class members.

The subject mentor was sensitive in introducing Alex to the class and ensured that his status was recognised in preparation for when he took this class. When Alex did take this class for the first time, the teaching assistant was drawn in to support the girl who had been identified whilst the boy was left on the periphery.

In discussion with the subject mentor, Alex asked if the teaching assistant could withdraw the 'troublesome' pupil to allow him to teach the other pupils without interruption. The withdrawn Traveller pupil was not so much of a concern to him.

Reflect upon alternative approaches to Alex's request. Take into consideration possible locations where this request might have been voiced.

Issues of classroom management, differentiation and managing support staff are implicated in this scenario. Each is grounded in a vast field of experience. Where should the subject mentor begin?

The teaching assistant plays a pivotal role in this scenario. How may this be harnessed for Alex's professional development?

Scenario 32

Richard

A mentor and class teacher discuss a dilemma they share. A highly respected trainee, Richard, assigned to the early years unit of a primary school, has asked if he may attend parent consultations in order to broaden his experience. In principle both staff members are in agreement about this, as they feel this is a vital part of the training they can offer.

However, it has reached the ears of the class teacher that Richard has spoken in very positive terms to one of the parents about the progress of their child in the unit. She has spoken to Richard, who confirmed that he was taken off his guard when he met the parent in the shopping precinct, and had been led by her words to confirm that the child was in fact 'extremely bright'. Other parents had seen this as a door opening and had sought Richard's assessments of their children. Unfortunately, Richard's 'assessment' of the first child did not concur with what the parents had been told by the class teacher and this fuelled conflict between the school and the family.

As the mentor and class teacher exchanged thoughts, they came to the decision that this incident could be turned into something quite positive in terms of Richard's progress. Already they had noticed that Richard's assessments of the pupils had been rather liberal. He did not seem to recognise when he had led them in his questioning, when they were using visual cues from others including his own non-verbal prompts. The balance between encouraging the pupils and the reliability of his assessments was brought into question. In observation he was equally liberal, verging on bias, particularly to those who were already achieving highly. Ongoing assessment through questioning, observation and learning conversations was important to this age of pupils; Richard would need to practise to expose his assumptions and possible sources of bias before presenting these to parents. The next time he would meet with parents to discuss progress would be in his first teaching post.

What sequence of events should the mentor and class teacher propose, given there are time constraints?

What are the implications for future practice and mentoring responsibilities?

Richard complains to the university tutor that he has been refused permission to attend the parent consultations. What are the possible courses open to the partnership and which will be most beneficial to Richard?

Scenario 33

Maya

Maya is a PGCE trainee in her first practice in a Year 5 class. The school has a high proportion of pupils for whom English is an additional language. Relations between school and community are good. Many of the classroom support assistants are drawn from the local community and some speak Punjabi, Gujarati or Urdu. There are two full-time assistants assigned to Year 5. Both are able to support the pupils in the class in mother tongue where necessary.

At the start of her practice Maya is confident in small group work and is now ready to teach the whole group. She knows she has prepared her lesson well and the teacher mentor has helped her to select appropriate resources. The class teacher's practice is to leave plans for the support assistants at the start of each day in their assigned boxes. Each assistant has a 'to and fro' book to report back on the progress of individuals to whom they have been directed. Maya follows the same pattern leaving the plan at the start of the day.

The teacher mentor observes the literacy lesson, where Maya exerts her control in a didactic manner. She moves through the introduction to her lesson as if in a monologue, rarely engaging the pupils even in eye contact. Pupils gaze ahead waiting to engage in the forthcoming directed activity. Maya issues instructions and the assistants move to ensure the pupils for whom English is an additional language have understood what is expected. Maya steps to the side, to the teacher's desk and waits. Both assistants converse frantically with the pupils in their groups, and Maya waits. The pupils work on until Maya comes to life and moves to the third part of the session. She leads the plenary involving one pupil who dictates her work which Maya writes on the board.

Secure in her relationship with the teacher mentor she opens the post-observation discussion: "I'm not doing this right. It's not that I'm not prepared, because I am. I spend ages planning but as soon as I stand in front of the class I just want to get to the end. I really feel so inadequate – shut out, almost. I have tremendous respect for the assistants and the work they do with the groups but don't know how to approach either of them or get to know those pupils. My background has been very much white European and I don't know where to begin. I don't understand how much support they really need or whether they need more encouragement to work in English. As soon as I stand in front of the class I feel isolated."

Take the role of the mentor and prioritise the issues with a timescale for actions. You will need to establish the time that may have elapsed and the time remaining on this practice. Prioritise the actions that should be taken to address the issue(s).

Had Maya not offered her self-evaluation, how might the scenario have unfolded?

How might the mentor facilitate Maya's learning through the teaching assistants?

The pupils appear to be compliant and do not challenge Maya. Had the pupils been more challenging, how might this have changed the mentor's approach to Maya?

Scenario 34

Lisa

On the tutor's first visit to the school there was optimism in the conversation between mentor, trainee and tutor.

On the second visit, prior to carrying out a joint observation, the tutor sensed an air of politeness, a circuitous route to the main points. The mentor in Lisa's presence reported that Lisa, in her final year, was unjustifiably lacking in confidence. "She's really doing very well with my babies and they are not making it easy for her."

Tutor and mentor observed Lisa in a literacy lesson, which was well structured, building appropriately on previous learning and using resources imaginatively. However, space was at a premium. There were some pupils who were distracting and interrupted the planned lesson.

In the post-observation discussion with the tutor, Lisa reflected well on her lesson and was quick to identify behaviour management as an area for her development: "I am really a confident person and I know I am well prepared, but I am never left alone with the class. Even when the mentor says she has to do something, she keeps coming in to check I am all right.

"I wouldn't mind if she just sat getting on with her work, because I know sometimes it is hard to find somewhere to go, but she keeps talking to the pupils, and it undermines my confidence. When parent helpers come in she always goes over to them and tells them what to do and I think I should do that.

"Last Tuesday she told me that some parents had approached her at the end of the day to say that they are not happy at the amount of non-qualified teaching contact the pupils are having. She says that she is anxious to avoid friction between the school and the parents so I am not to speak with the parents any more. She will take responsibility for receiving and dismissing them each day as if I am not here. I mean, I know she's got a point and she is supportive but sometimes I feel as if she gives with one hand and takes with the other.

"I feel I'm quite creative and would love to make an interactive display, but I've been afraid to in case the distractible pupils use it as another reason for not conforming. On top of that we have little space – you saw how I juggled with bookstands, the whiteboard and flipcharts. If I want the pupils to be interactive they have to tread on others to get to the front. Pupils who don't like to be squashed sit around the edge and wriggle, then get attention from others and the disruption starts all over again. The mentor has seen it and says she understands but I feel frustrated. I'll get through to the end because I'm determined."

Trainee and mentor are mutually dependent, defined by each other's success or otherwise. The mentor's role is to balance multiple responsibilities which are evidenced in this scenario and lead the trainee in professional development. Analyse the detail of this scenario and reconstruct it to counter the potential barriers to Lisa's development.

As an advanced mentor, what action would you take to improve the performance of this mentor?

As an advanced mentor, what strategies would you use to work with schools where mentors:

- were unwilling to mentor;
- were reluctant to give sufficient time to mentor;
- felt inadequate in their mentoring skills?

(In providing some solutions to the problems, check the skills the advanced mentor and mentors would demonstrate against the TDA Eastern Region Mentor Levels 1–3 Descriptors and Performance Criteria in Appendix 1.)

Chapter 5

The craft of mentoring in schools

Bridget Hoad

Introduction

This chapter gives some theoretical insights into the nature of mentoring in schools for those who wish to explore this further. It begins by defining mentoring and outlining the roles of the mentor. It then examines the **process** of being a mentor from both trainee and mentor perspectives. Issues associated with mentoring such as reflection, reflexivity and becoming a critical practitioner are explored together with power relations, articulation of pedagogical skills, autonomy and interdependency. The **actions** mentors take are described through the setting of the learning conversation. Issues such as race, gender and disability are considered within this context. Finally there is a move towards developing a model whereby mentor and trainee negotiate the realities of practice, and mentor and co-mentors recursively develop their professional roles.

Legislation in the form of the DFE Circular 9/92 (DFE 1992) contributed to the pivotal role of mentoring in ITT. Postgraduate trainees were directed to spend two thirds of their one-year course in school-based activities. This followed a growing and continuing body of evidence that highlighted the potential for learning through social participation of novices alongside 'expert' practitioners (Vygotsky, 1987; Lave and Wenger, 1991; Rogoff, 1995).

The mentor role

Mentor in Greek mythology was the trusted friend of Ulysses who took responsibility for educating the son of Ulysses, Telemachus, in his absence. His name has become a synonym for 'instructor and guide'. Trust, instruction and guidance continue to be highly valued in mentoring relationships.

The term 'mentoring' describes 'the support given by one (usually more experienced) person for the growth and learning of another, and for their integration into and acceptance by a specific community (Malderez, 2001, p.57).

In a dynamic, reciprocal relationship the mentor facilitates the development of the trainee as s/he grows from novice to full practitioner, nurturing and challenging through a full range of responsibilities, thus linking theory to practice. The mentoring role is developmental and only by engaging in it can it be learned. Just as the mentor nurtures the trainee, the mentor should be nurtured and supported.

The professional mentor, as opposed to the subject mentor or class teacher mentor, has a distinct role which will afford a differing perspective on mentoring. The professional mentor's responsibilities include:

- Devising an induction programme;
- Briefing subject mentors and agreeing a programme of school-based training with them;
- Channelling communications between all partners;
- Devising and co-ordinating a school-based programme in liaison with the link tutor to connect with the higher education institution (HEI) based part of the course;
- Being responsible for and co-ordinating a school-based programme;
- Facilitating discussions with trainees about aspects of the teacher's role and school life;
- Devising and providing a professional programme to include content such as legal responsibilities, policies, responsibilities of governors, applying for jobs and opportunities for involvement in whole school life (Capel, 2003, p.138).

The mentor's responsibilities include:

- Informing trainees about the ability ranges of the groups of pupils;
- Sharing set procedures in the department;
- Sharing resources;
- Supporting trainees in target setting and advising about alternative strategies;
- Monitoring the development of trainees' teaching files (planning and monitoring, assessment, recording, reporting and accountability);

- Planning and delivering collaborative teaching activities;
- Discussing trainees' lesson plans and evaluations and advising appropriately;
- Observing trainees teaching and providing constructive feedback;
- Supporting trainees in reflection and analysis of their practice;
- Providing written feedback on practice (Capel, 2003, p.138).

In the secondary sector the professional mentor and subject mentor collaborate jointly and with the tutor (who may or may not be a subject tutor). A similar pattern may be reflected in the primary and early years sectors. Here a teacher may be appointed who takes on the role of professional mentor, but the professional mentor may sometimes be the headteacher. Both professional mentor and class teacher mentor will contribute to the professional development of the trainee, linking with the tutor. In other examples in the primary and early years sectors the class teacher mentor will have day to day contact with the trainee and will be responsible for the monitoring and paperwork associated with ITT, supported by the tutor. This diverse organisation of school-based mentoring will lead to varied and valuable perspectives on mentoring.

McIntyre,1997, suggested that in broad terms the tutor and HEI (and any other ITT provider) are responsible for research and theory-based knowledge, whilst the school-based mentors contribute to situated knowledge of teaching, learning and practical perspectives. This over-generalised view implies a dichotomy in the trainees' experiences which in practice is not so clearly defined.

The trainee's view of mentoring

Hobson, 2002, showed that trainees perceive school-based mentoring to be a if not the key element of ITT experience. In researching with PGCE trainees, Hobson found a high degree of satisfaction with the effectiveness of school-based mentors.

Trainees have expressed their major concern in training as the ability to manage pupils and maintain discipline (Tomlinson et al, 1996; TES, 29 July 2005). Hobson found that school-based mentors were regarded more effective than any other ITT personnel in helping them to develop in this area (p.8). The same trainees rated school-based mentors most effective in assisting them to develop a range of teaching methods. Feedback and constructive criticism given by mentors following observed teaching was centrally important to them in the process of learning teaching. Trainees disliked it when the onus was placed on them to ask for help if experiencing problems, when classroom practices did not reflect current thinking, where written records of observations, progress or targets were lacking, where there were breaks in communication between the ITT personnel and where there were personality clashes (pp.9–13).

Mee-Lee and Bush, 2003, surveyed mentors and mentees to discover their perceptions of the desirable characteristics of mentors. The top four rankings indicated that an understanding and sympathetic mentor was most important, followed by one who was accessible to mentees. A good communicator ranked third, and enthusiasm for the role ranked fourth. Commitment to the overall experience of mentoring was clearly important.

The mentor's view of mentoring

The mentor–trainee relationship is one of mutual trust. For the mentor, teaching adults may be a new experience and one which demands building trust within a short space of time. Von Glaserfeld, 1996, was concerned with the need for the 'expert' to appreciate the viewpoint of the 'novice', and this is relevant both to pupils and adult learners:

> Students perceive their environment in ways that may be very different from those intended by educators... This emphasises the teacher's need to construct a hypothetical model of the particular conceptual worlds of the students they are facing. One can hope to induce changes in their way of thinking only if one has some inkling as to the domains of experience, the concepts and the conceptual relations the students possess at the moment (Von Glaserfeld, 1996, p.7).

Where mentors are committed in sharing time, they have the opportunity to be enlightened by the experiences of the trainee. At the same time the trainees value the school-based mentor who is 'supportive, reassuring, prepared and able to make time for them, to offer practical advice and ideas relating to their teaching, and to provide constructive feedback on their teaching attempts' (Hobson, 2002, p.16).

Time invested leads to a mutual sense of being valued. However, the overwhelming demands of school life and juggling of priorities may constrain building such relationships (Maynard, 1996, p.115). Trainees may have attitudes and approaches that present barriers to relationship building. Their desire to be seen as competent teachers may limit their willingness to be seen as a learner – a 'novice' (Edwards, 1998). The mentor has to reconcile the demands upon time with coming to understand the realities of the trainees' world.

To assist trainees in developing effective teaching strategies, mentors may model their own strategies. If modelling is supported by articulation of how they teach and why one approach is more appropriate than another in a particular context, then the teaching and learning is likely to be more effective. Often practised teacher mentors find it difficult to articulate in this way because their strategies have become instinctive. At this point the mentor engages in reflection, reflexivity and becoming a critical practitioner.

Schon, 1983, outlined three levels of reflection: reflection in practice which entails moment to moment assessments and adaptations; reflection on practice which involves evaluation of past actions to suggest what might be appropriate actions in similar situations; and reflection for practice which is concerned with planning for future actions, learning from successes and errors. In the classroom a trainee might have had to respond to an unscheduled interruption which unsettled some of the pupils (reflection in practice). In discussion with the mentor following the session the trainee might discuss whether s/he should have tried to continue with the lesson plan or allowed an unscheduled break (reflection on practice). Together they might discuss the implications of each possibility and agree a practice for the future (reflection for practice).

Elliott, 1993, describes the reflexive practitioner whose reflections on classroom practice go beyond the immediate situation to reflect upon the effect of institutional structures. The self as co-participant in that institution is included in the reflections, interrogating the teacher's own beliefs, assumptions and prejudices on which the teaching is grounded. Here the mentor and trainee might bring their reflections to a wider audience and consider the impact of whole school policies. For example, an incident of bullying may have highlighted an inadequacy in the school's anti-bullying policy. In reviewing the policy, the teacher mentor might be drawn to question self-beliefs and whether s/he is willing to implement proposals put forward in the review. At the same time s/he knows the strength of the policy will rely upon consistent implementation by all staff, including trainees.

Carr and Kemmis, 1986, take reflection and reflexivity a step further to encompass political, ideological and social process. The critical practitioner interrogates the processes which frame education and exposes, for example, inequalities in power and discriminatory practices in race, gender and disability. The critical practitioner as mentor will be aware of the hierarchical, dyadic relationship with the trainee and will seek to construct a mutually beneficial relationship. Where social and cultural differences exist these will be valued and capitalised on.

To become a reflective, reflexive or critical practitioner it is necessary to stand back and make a rational analysis. The mentor may have an 'ideal trainee', an 'ideal pupil', and will examine how these ideals have come about. Conscious actions and unconscious processes may be difficult to articulate to another as has been said, yet true reflection grapples with these through discursive interactions. The learning conversations held between mentor and trainee are mutually constituting and allow both to voice what they know and discover what they yet need to find out.

Interdependency, the desire not to let anyone down, drives the actions of reflection and reflexivity. The mentor reflects to interrogate his or her strategies in response to the individual needs of the trainee and the social contexts in which those needs are expressed. As a result of those reflections, trainee and mentor are changed and shaped, empowering them both through learning.

The roles of the mentor include those concerned with induction into the school community and classroom cultures. Here expectations are created and future behaviours are shaped. Loyalty, commitment and productivity are engendered through the induction process. The mentor holds the 'expert' knowledge of routines, procedures and aims but, reflecting the interdependency of each, shares this with the trainee so that both may strive towards autonomy.

Mentors play a key role in the trainee's growing identity as a teacher. They provide emotional and psychological support. Sivan and Chan, 2003, draw attention to the changing needs of trainees as they gain experience (p.191). They found when they studied novice and more experienced trainees that novices tend to be more concerned with their own identities as teachers, often filled with self-doubt. The novice trainee may have acquired skills in planning effectively but may not have acquired the repertoire of strategies needed to carry the plans through to practice. As the trainees gain confidence they expect more guidance on pedagogical issues related to their teaching skills and their pupils' learning. With the growth of identity comes the interest in transferable skills. The committed mentor then should also be responsive to individual trainees' experiences, developmental levels and interests.

Evans et al, 1996, found that teacher mentors in schools regarded mentoring as 'subordinate to what they perceived as their primary role of teaching' (pp.147–9). Many mentors defined their own success by the success of their trainees (Gilles and Wilson, 2004, p.101). The role of mentor is developmental and as such demands independence and ingenuity. A mentor unsupported may feel isolated and insecure. The situated nature of the job means it is constantly evolving as decisions are made: when to intervene, when to allow a lesson to be learned from a bad judgement, when to offer unconditional support, when to challenge. Acknowledging these points, the benefits to the mentor of working with the adult trainee outweigh the constraints.

Mentors extend their teaching and learning skills beyond the pupils they usually encounter to working with adults. They provide valuable insights for programme planners through their partnership with HEIs. These learning relationships lead to enhanced interpersonal skills (Ackley and Gall, 1992; Stevens, 1999; Zachary, 2000, cited in Gilles and Wilson, 2004, p.91). Trainees bring to the relationship new ideas and theories which update the mentor in current thinking. Their critical reflections, training and learning lead to enhanced professional opportunities (Stevens, 1999). Their pivotal roles extend outside the classroom, but the site of their development is the classroom, and particularly the setting for the learning conversation.

The **process** of becoming a mentor has been discussed and now we turn to the **actions** mentors take.

Conducting learning conversations

Learning conversations may take place informally as day to day matters occur, or formally as planning meetings, monitoring following observation or target setting. In both situations the site and timing set the arena for a positive outcome. Timetabled meetings formalise the contract between mentor and trainee, give a sense of belonging and are part of the social context in which the trainee's identity is embedded. As a social structure, meetings between mentor and trainee (and tutor) involve relations of power and the aim must be to empower the novice.

Beliefs, understandings, skills, attitudes and dispositions to work and learning are brought to the learning conversation by mentor and trainee. Each makes adjustments to the other and is changed by the other, but the onus to 'fit in' is with the newcomer. The teaching staff and the mentor are familiar with routines and histories, have control over resources, and the organisation of work. This control may be used to empower or disempower the trainee. The timing and conduct of the learning conversations will reflect the power relations. Where networks of mentors are involved with trainees, negotiation of power is yet more complex, with further hierarchical layers. Mentors are usually selected for the trainee rather than by the trainee, so both need to work towards constructing trust and mutual respect through learning conversations.

The elation of success and the discomfort of 'failure' both find expression in these conversations. Trainee narratives following teaching may look for causal explanations outside themselves to account for perceived failure. They may locate themselves in an image of a teacher which they cannot yet realise. As a result the pupils may become the explanation for their apparent inadequacy. To avoid further public 'failings', they become entrenched in a 'safe' model of teaching which does not motivate or challenge the pupils. The situation is likely to be self-perpetuating without the sensitive intervention of the mentor.

Such tensions and contradictions are to be resolved in the learning conversation, and this is most difficult when issues lie covertly between mentor and trainee. An open climate should be fostered where discussions around issues are welcomed. Issues of race, gender, or disability should not be sidestepped nor allowed to become a focus to the detriment of candid discussion. Johnson-Bailey and Cervero, 2004, outline the historical domination in cross-cultural mentoring, the domination of blacks by whites. They maintain that 'the dyadic paternalistic hierarchical nature of the mentoring process resembles the authoritative superior and the deferential subordinate that is a painful part of the racist legacy' (p.15).

Whilst mentors would do well to be aware of these possibilities, it is worth noting that the cross-cultural dimension of race could be reversed! Also, the learning conversations may productively capitalise on the potential for diversity outcomes for the mutual benefit of pupils, mentor, school and trainee.

In either case, explicit discussion of potential barriers to professional development breaks down those barriers and grants access to psychosocial support. When racism is evident amongst the pupils, the mentor must discharge the legal duty 'to be proactive in promoting racial equality' (The Race Relations [Amendment] Act 2000). Cole and Stuart, 2005, looked at the experiences of British Asian and black, and overseas trainee teachers in the south-east of England. Trainees reported that whilst overt noticed and reported racist remarks from pupils were strictly dealt with, covert racism was not addressed (p.357). Pupils who may not have much experience with minority ethnic people should have positive experiences with regard to ethnicity, and the trainee could be an asset in this, developing both curricular and extra-curricular activities. In learning conversations the mentor has an obligation to monitor and protect the trainee with positive use of the power invested in him or her.

Power in the learning conversation is derived from the experience of the 'more knowledgeable other'. Vygotsky, 1987, described the social construction of learning whereby the 'expert' scaffolds learning for the novice and contingently withdraws the support offered. Lave and Wenger, 1991, outline legitimate peripheral participation when learners work together with masters in legitimate peripheral activity – peripheral because they work in a limited way with limited responsibility but observing the master at work. Both master and learner participate in discussion negotiating meanings and improvise to solve problems. The master cautiously withdraws as s/he shares common understanding with the learner. The learner becomes more competent – the observation is mutual, the outcome mutually beneficial.

Competency involves both conceptual and practical knowledge. Practical knowledge is modelled and demonstrated in action. Procedures such as transitions within lessons and commanding attention may be mirrored for the trainee. Conceptual knowledge is grounded in practice and constructed through learning conversations whereby the trainee comes to understand the reasons for decisions or approaches to solving problems. In discourse both trainee and mentor are prompted to describe the mental models on which they base decisions. Observation and reflective narratives are vehicles for exposing and recognising conceptual knowledge. Through learning conversations, the mentor assesses the effectiveness of the opportunities offered to the trainee. Activities and target setting move the trainee from dependence on the mentor to independent decision making and problem solving, from the periphery of practice to the centre.

The learning conversation is central to the pivotal role of the mentor. Communication between mentors where there is a network is as vital as communication between mentor and trainee. Figure 1 shows those avenues of communication. The mentor's role is to offer practical knowledge and psychosocial support, skills and subject knowledge and conceptual knowledge. This is facilitated through induction, learning conversations and reflective narratives, through modelling, demonstration and instruction and through discursive meetings, planning, assessment and evaluation respectively. The action of engagement leads to reflexivity and the development of a critical practitioner. The outcomes are shared with and come about through interaction with colleagues as well as the trainee. The whole is mutually supporting.

The unique and individual characteristics of each mentoring partnership are reflected in the various models of mentoring to which interested readers may refer. For example, Saunders et al, 1995, interviewed twenty-nine mentors and found four typologies: *the hands-off facilitator* who emphasises discussion, praise and challenge; *the collaborative mentor* who actively works alongside trainees in a more continuous way; *the professional friend* who provides access to the full range of school experience and becomes involved as necessary; and *the classical mentor* who emphasises counselling and feedback in a relatively reactive process. Some other models of mentoring to which the reader might refer are: Yeomans and Sampson, 1994; Maynard and Furlong, 1993; Elliott and Calderhead, 1993.

In summary, the learning conversation is the vehicle through which professional development is facilitated. The timing and situation in which this takes place are as important to the effectiveness of this conversation as the skills that the mentor – and trainee – bring to it. The models of mentoring which are adopted will be influenced by the unique experiences of the mentor, the structures and ethos within the school and the developmental needs of the trainee.

Conclusion

Mentoring is a process of becoming: a continuous development. The skills of reflection, reflexivity and becoming a critical practitioner are paramount within the mentoring relationship. These lead the mentor to question such issues as power relations, gender, race and disability within the adult partnership. This partnership develops and is developed by the professional roles played out by each participant.

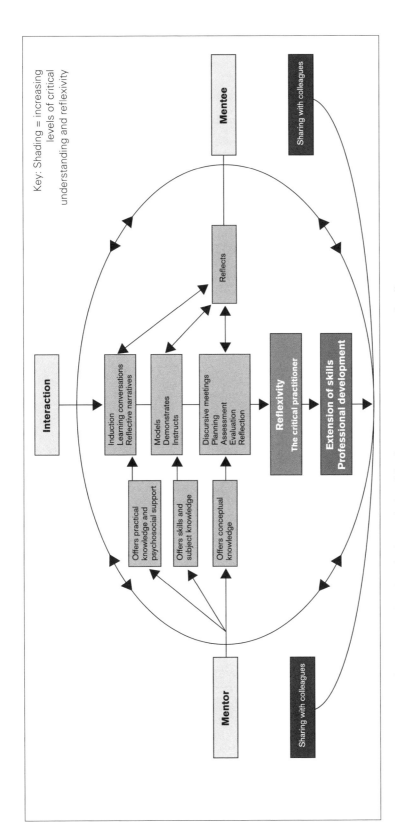

Figure 1: A model of mentoring showing the interrelationships between mentor, mentee and colleagues

 **University of Hertfordshire** | *working in partnership to promote excellence in teacher education*

Appendix 1: Mentor levels

TDA Eastern Region ITT providers: standards for mentor training: as evidence for performance management review, etc.

Level descriptors for mentors

Level 1: A totally new mentor, someone in their first year of mentoring or one who has mentored one trainee with support from a more experienced colleague.

Evidence of operating at Level 1: supporting a trainee, as above, and
- ❖ writing the required paperwork (i.e. observation reports, target setting, interim/final reports, references) for the ITT provider;
- ❖ attending mentor training focused on Level 1 criteria (provided by HEI/SCITT/other provider) that will probably be institution- and phase-specific.

Level 2: An experienced, confident mentor who has mentored one or more trainees effectively over a substantial and sustained teaching practice using the QTS Standards. Is able to contribute to supporting other mentors within the school and possibly in a wider context, e.g. in another school, in other classes in own school, in helping to deliver training for the ITT provider or mentoring NQTs. Evidence of reaching this level may contribute to a UPS2/AST portfolio.

Evidence of operating at Level 2: supporting a variety of trainees, including:
- ❖ completion of a range of paperwork (i.e. observation reports, target setting, interim/final reports, references);
- ❖ involvement in professional development opportunities at (certificated) Level 2 with a focus on the further development of effective ITT mentoring;
- ❖ having written and delivered feedback and targets from a joint lesson observation in the school setting **or** having written a reflective log on a particular topic **or** having written a report on what has been done to support a new mentor **or** having written a report on the active engagement with another's professional development **or** involvement in the delivery of Level 1 mentor training and a written critique of this training.

Level 3: Additionally to Level 2, Level 3 is an advanced mentor who is able to manage other mentors as a professional mentor/ITT co-ordinator. Is likely to be working at Masters level on an accredited programme of study and understand the concepts and theories underpinning the principles and practices of mentoring. This mentor may be applying their mentoring expertise in settings external to their own school. Evidence of reaching this level may contribute to a UPS3 or NPQH portfolio.

Evidence of operating at Level 3:
- ❖ CATs accredited assignment;
- ❖ history of attending and providing professional development in ITT;
- ❖ working closely with local school cluster/HEI.

These performance criteria for mentors and the related documentation were outlined and agreed by members of the TDA Eastern Region Steering Committee in 2005-6. They provide a mechanism for identifying and documenting the extensive and high level skills used and developed by mentors when supporting teacher trainees. Further work is being done by the originators to pilot and build on this documentation.

Origin: Punter, Pickering, Miles, Leverett, Taylor, Osborne, Amrane-Cooper, Coltman, Warwick
TDA Eastern Region Steering Committee

Performance criteria for mentors: Expectations, responsibilities and professional requirements

LEVEL 1

Mentor Name: ... ... School: ... ...

Pre-requisites as a teacher	Head's/Prof Mentor's signature
Model professional behaviour in all aspects of work, including: ❖ knowledge of teachers' responsibilities; ❖ an inclusive commitment to trainees' development; ❖ a willingness to engage in professional dialogue with trainees.	
Have good subject knowledge including NCPoS, strategies and exam syllabuses.	
Have knowledge of the work of professional bodies.	
Provide a model of effective classroom practice and support in: ❖ planning; ❖ managing the classroom and pupils; ❖ managing other adults; ❖ using a range of teaching styles to support learning styles; ❖ identifying pupils' achievement and progression; ❖ managing equal opportunities and inclusion issues.	
Be able to provide information on professional bodies.	
Know how to assess and moderate pupils' work.	

GTC TLA verification criteria as objectives	As a **mentor within the school setting**, the **success criteria** are to:	Tutor's signature
Demonstrate knowledge of professional practice, current relevant sources and appropriate referencing.	Be familiar with the QTS Standards.	
	Know the trainee's programme requirements.	
Identify and access peer support in mentoring. Be clear about the value of the support and how this will move on teachers' development.	Know the principles of partnership and liaise effectively with the ITT provider.	
	Be briefed/trained.	
	Possess good communication and interpersonal skills.	
	Recognise the dual support and assessment role of the mentor.	
	Liaise with other colleagues to support the trainee's subject and pedagogical knowledge.	
Plan the professional learning/training and set aims, targets, timescales and progression.	Plan and implement the training programme, with attention paid to the trainee's records/audits.	
Carry out change – implement, review, monitor, analyse and evaluate progress.	Complete the appropriate paperwork.	
	Assess trainees by: ❖ undertaking analytical lesson observations and giving formative feedback; ❖ assessing, using a range of evidence, in relation to the Standards; ❖ supporting the trainee in setting appropriate targets; ❖ evaluating progress.	
Evaluate and disseminate good practice.	Recognise the value of mentoring in CPD.	
	Support trainees in generalising from specific experiences in the classroom.	
	Understand and develop effective professional relationships with adult learners and discuss good practice.	

Signed: University of Hertfordshire Tutor: ... ... Date: ... ...

Signed: Professional Mentor/Headteacher: ... ...

Origin: Punter, Pickering, Miles, Leverett, Taylor, Osborne, Amrane-Cooper, Coltman, Warwick
TDA Eastern Region Steering Committee

Mentor Name: ... ...

GTC TLA verification criteria as objectives (Level 2 differentiated objectives in bold)	As a **mentor within the school setting**, the **success criteria** are to:
Demonstrate knowledge of professional practice, current relevant sources and appropriate referencing. **Undertake an analysis of the additional knowledge and ideas and of how these impact on teacher development.**	❖ Understand the ways in which mentors can contribute to partnership development.
Identify and access peer support in mentoring. Be clear about the value of the support and how this will move on teachers' development. **Do this over time; critically analyse the impact upon teachers' development.**	❖ Understand how to facilitate trainees' self-evaluation and reflection. ❖ Engage with and help to resolve sensitive issues for trainees. ❖ Be able to reflect critically on their own and others' practice for professional development.
Plan the professional learning/training and set aims, targets, timescales and progression. **A coherent plan to be developed and key learning opportunities to be identified with outcomes.**	❖ Understand the progression of professional development during a training programme. ❖ Ensure that trainees are working with good role models in school.
Carry out change – implement, review, monitor, analyse and evaluate progress. **Identify further actions and learning required, reflect upon actions and outcomes.**	❖ Use assessment procedures for trainees confidently and consistently to ensure progression. ❖ Moderate trainees within own school. ❖ Ensure effective external moderation/ examination procedures are followed. ❖ Provide effective feedback and set targets to ensure progression; in particular be able to address the developmental needs of challenging trainees, e.g. referrals/ those at risk of failure, very good trainees, those who have ceased to progress.
Evaluate and disseminate good practice **through sharing with immediate colleagues. Critical reflection and analysis help to identify next steps.**	❖ Be involved in training new mentors within their own school/elsewhere.

Satisfactory written unit of work submitted (1,000 words max, see overleaf for alternatives)

Signed Headteacher/Professional Mentor: ... ...

Origin: Punter, Pickering, Miles, Leverett, Taylor, TDA Eastern Region

responsibilities and professional requirements

School: …

Level 2 evidence	Professional skills for teachers within the Standards framework (in draft form at the time of publication)				NPQH
	Induction/ main scale teachers (I) should:	Post threshold teachers (P) should:	Excellent teachers (E) should:	Advanced skills teachers (A) should:	
Workshop attendance		P11 Contribute to the professional development of colleagues through coaching and mentoring, demonstrating effective practice, and providing advice and feedback.			Establish systems for monitoring and evaluating the quality of teaching and learning.
Workshop attendance					
Workshop attendance			E13 Contribute to the professional development of colleagues using a broad range of techniques and skills appropriate to their needs so that they demonstrate enhanced and effective practice.		Plan and support the work of individual staff.
Workshop attendance					
Assignment written/oral					Ensure that trainees and NQTs are appropriately trained, monitored, supported and assessed.
Assignment written/oral			E14 Make well-founded appraisals of situations on which they are asked to advise, applying high level skills in classroom observation to evaluate and advise colleagues on their work and devising and implementing effective strategies to meet the learning needs of children and young people leading to improvements in pupil outcomes.		
Assignment written/oral					
Assignment written/oral				A3 Possess the analytical, interpersonal and organisational skills necessary to work effectively with staff and leadership teams beyond their own school.	Support and co-ordinate the provision of high quality professional development.
Partnership Director/ Head to sign					Take action to improve the performance of staff.

Date: … … … … … … … … … … … … … … … …

Signed Director of Partnership, School of Education: … … … … … … … … … … … … … … … … … …

Osborne, Amrane-Cooper, Coltman, Warwick
Steering Committee

GTC TLA verification criteria as objectives (Level 3 differentiated objectives in bold)	As a **contributor to ITT in a context wider than one school** the **success criteria** are to:
<u>Demonstrate knowledge</u> of professional practice, current relevant sources and appropriate referencing. Undertake an analysis of the additional knowledge and ideas and of how these impact on teacher development. **Use critical analysis, synthesis of concepts and theories and practice. AND** <u>Evaluate and disseminate</u> good practice through sharing with immediate colleagues. Critical reflection and analysis help to identify next steps. **This is shared with immediate colleagues and a wider audience. Critical reflection and analysis have included how to develop further.**	Demonstrate a commitment to partnership development beyond the one school context, e.g. interviewing, programme development. Contribute to taught courses on ITT beyond the one school. Be involved in training new mentors in a wider ITT context.
<u>Identify and access peer support</u> in mentoring. Be clear about the value of the support and how this will move on teachers' development. Do this over time; critically analyse the impact upon teachers' development. **Sustained application. Referencing to the theoretical and practical knowledge base.**	Be able to link theory and practice.
<u>Plan the professional learning/training</u> and set aims, targets, timescales and progression. A coherent plan to be developed and key learning opportunities to be identified with outcomes. **Give a rationale referenced to relevant knowledge, set up a planned programme and take account of the implications.**	Contribute to the development of materials to be disseminated within/beyond the partnership provider.
<u>Carry out change</u> – implement, review, monitor, analyse and evaluate progress. Identify further actions and learning required; reflect upon actions and outcomes. **Reflection is a key approach.**	Assess trainees by moderating beyond own school context.

Origin: Punter, Pickering, Miles, Leverett, Taylor, TDA Eastern Region

responsibilities and professional requirements

Level 3 evidence	Professional competences in relation to: UPS 2, 3, AST, NPQH
CATs accredited module at Masters level	**AST:** Commitment to outreach work. **NPQH:** Develop effective links in the local community. Extend network of contacts with other educational bodies. **AST:** Have highly developed interpersonal skills which allow them to be effective in schools and situations other than their own. Lead CPD.
CATs accredited module at Masters level	**AST:** Analyse teaching and know how improvements can be made.
CATs accredited module at Masters level	**AST:** Lead the development of school-based ITT.
CATs accredited module at Masters level	**Headteacher:** Maintain liaison with other schools and higher education. Support and co-ordinate the provision of high quality professional development.

Appendix 2
Roger Levy

A reading list to support continuing professional development

General texts, often covering more than one specific aspect on mentoring and coaching

Arthur, J., Davison, J. and Moss, J., *Subject Mentoring in the Secondary School*, London: Kogan Page, 1997

Brockbank, A. and McGill, I., *Facilitating Reflective Learning in Higher Education*, Buckingham: Open University Press, 1998

Brooks, V. and Sikes, P. with Husbands, C., *The Good Mentor Guide*, Buckingham: OUP, 1997

Campbell, A. and Kane, I., *School-Based Teacher Education: Telling Tales from a Fictional Primary School*, London: David Fulton, 1998

DFES, *Teachers' Standards Framework: Helping You Develop*, London: DFES, 2001

Edwards, A. and Collison, J., *Mentoring and Developing Practice in Primary Schools*, Buckingham: OUP, 1996

Fish, D., *Quality Mentoring for Student Teachers: A Principled Approach to Practice*, London: David Fulton, 1995

Fletcher, S., *Mentoring in Schools*, London: Kogan Page, 2000

Grimmett, P.P., Erickson, G., MacKinnon, A.M. and Riechen, T.J., 'Reflective practice in teacher education', in Clift, R.T., Houston R.W. and Pugarch, M.C. (eds), *Encouraging Reflective Practice in Education: An Analysis of Issues and Programs*, New York: Teachers College Press, 1990

Kerry, T. and Shelton Mayes, A., *Issues in Mentoring*, London: Routledge,1995

Maynard, T. (ed.), *An Introduction to Primary Mentoring*, London: Cassell, 1997

Maynard, T., 'The limits of mentoring: the contribution of the Higher Education tutor to primary student teachers' school-based learning', in Furlong, J. and Smith, R. (eds), *The Role of Higher Education in Initial Teacher Training*, London: Kogan Page, 1996, pp.101–18

McIntyre, D. and Hagger, H., 'Teachers' expertise and models of mentoring', in McIntyre, D., Hagger, H. and Wilkin, M. (eds), *Mentoring: Perspectives on School-Based Teacher Education*, London: Kogan Page, 1993, pp.86–102

McIntyre, D. and Hagger, H., *Mentors in Schools: Developing the Profession of Teaching*, London: David Fulton, 1996

McIntyre, D., Hagger, H. and Wilkin, M. (eds), *Mentoring: Perspectives on School-Based Teacher Education*, London: Kogan Page, 1993

McIntyre, D. (ed.), *Teacher Education Research in a New Context: The Oxford Internship Scheme*, London: Paul Chapman, 1997

Shaw, R., *Teacher Training in Secondary Schools*, London: Kogan Page, 2nd edn, 1996

Smith, P. and West-Burnham, J. (eds), *Mentoring in the Effective School*, London: Longman, 1993

Tomlinson, P., *Understanding Mentoring: Reflective Strategies for School-Based Teacher Preparation*, Buckingham: OUP, 1995

Wilkin, M. (ed.), *Mentoring in Schools*, London: Kogan Page, 1992

Wilkin, M. and Sankey, D. (eds), *Collaboration and Transition in Initial Teacher Training*, London: Kogan Page, 1994

Williams, A.E. (ed.), *Perspectives on Partnership*, London: Falmer Press, 1994

Williams, A.E. (ed.), *Partnership in Secondary Initial Teacher Education*, London: David Fulton, 1995

Yeomans, R. and Sampson, J., *Mentoring in the Primary School*, London: Falmer Press, 1994

Handbooks/resources

Dharesh, J.C., *Teachers Mentoring Teachers: A Practical Approach to helping New and Inexperienced Staff*, Thousand Oaks, CA: Corwin Press, 2003

Geen, A., *A Practical Guide to Mentoring: Developing Initial Teacher Education and Training in Schools*, Arthur Geen, 2002

Hagger, H., Burn, K. and McIntyre, D., *The School Mentor Handbook: Essential Skills and Strategies for Working with Student Teachers*, London: Kogan Page, 1993

Kajs, L.T., 'Framework for Designing a Mentoring Program for Novice Teachers', *Mentoring and tutoring*, Vol. 10, No. 1, 2002, pp.57–69

Kenward, H., *An Induction Manual for Newly Qualified and Returning Teachers*, London: David Fulton, 2001

Maynard, T. and Furlong, J., 'Learning to teach and models of mentoring', in McIntyre, D., Hagger, H. and Wilkin, M. (eds), *Mentoring: Perspectives on School-Based Teacher Education*, London: Kogan Page, 1993, pp.69–85

Stephens, P., *Essential Mentoring Skills: A Practical Handbook for School-Based Teacher Educators*, Cheltenham: Stanley Thornes, 1996

TTA, *Supporting Induction for Newly Qualified Teachers*, London: TTA, 1999

Watkins, C. and Whalley, C., *Mentoring: Resources for School-based Development*, London: Longman, 1993

Wilkin, M., Furlong, J. and Maynard, T., *The Subject Mentor Handbook for the Secondary School*, London: Kogan Page, 1997

Mentee development

Burn, K., Everton, T., Hagger, H. and Mutton, T., 'The complex development of student-teachers' thinking', *Teachers and Teaching: Theory and Practice*, Vol. 9, No. 4, 2003, pp.309–31

Conway, P.F. and Clark, C.M., 'The journey inward and outward: a re-examination of Fuller's concerns-based model of teacher development', *Teaching and Teacher Education*, Vol. 19, No. 5, 2003, pp.465–82

Dreyfus, H.L. and Dreyfus, S.E., *Mind Over Machine*, New York: Free Press, 1986

Elliott, B. and Calderhead, J., 'Mentoring for teacher development: possibilities and caveats', in McIntyre, D., Hagger, H., and Wilkin, M. (eds), *Mentoring: Perspectives on School-Based Teacher Education*, London: Kogan Page, 1993, pp.54–67

Fuller, F.F., 'Concerns of teachers: a developmental conceptualisation', *American Educational Research Journal*, 6, pp.207-226, 1969, pp.207–26

Furlong, J. and Maynard, T., *Mentoring Student Teachers: The Growth of Professional Knowledge*, London: Routledge, 1995

Harvard, G. and Dunne, R., 'The role of the mentor in developing teacher competence', *Westminster Studies in Education*, Vol. 15, No. 1, 1992, pp.33–44

Maynard, T. and Furlong, J., 'Learning to teach and models of mentoring', in McIntyre, D., Hagger, H. and Wilkin, M. (eds), *Mentoring: Perspectives on School-Based Teacher Education*, London: Kogan Page, 1993, pp.69–85

Shulman, L.S. and Shulman, J.H., 'How and what teachers learn: a shifting perspective', *Journal of Curriculum Studies*, Vol. 36, No. 2, 2004, pp.257–71

Tann, S., 'Supporting the student teacher in the classroom', in Wilkin, M. and Sankey, D. (eds), *Collaboration and Transition in Initial Teacher Training*, London: Kogan Page, 1994, pp.94–106

Mentor/coach mentees

Braund, M., 'Helping primary student teachers understand pupils' learning: exploring the student-mentor interaction', *Mentoring and tutoring*, Vol. 9, No. 3, 2001, pp.189–200

Bullough, R.V. and Draper, R., 'Making sense of a failed triad: mentors, university supervisors, and positioning theory', *Journal of Teacher Education*, Vol. 55, No. 5, 2004, pp.407–20

Field, K., 'You and your mentor', *Mentoring and tutoring*, Vol. 4, No. 3, 1997, pp.25–32

Furlong, J. and Maynard, T., *Mentoring Student Teachers: The Growth of Professional Knowledge*, London: Routledge, 1997

Tang, S.Y.F., 'Challenge and support: the dynamics of student teachers' professional learning in the field experience', *Teaching and Teacher Education*, 19, 2003, pp.483–98

Tann, S., 'Supporting the student teacher in the classroom', in Wilkin, M. and Sankey, D. (eds), *Collaboration and Transition in Initial Teacher Training*, London: Kogan Page, 1994, pp.94–106

Zanting, A., Verloop, N. and Vermunt, J.D., 'How do teachers elicit their mentor teachers' practical knowledge', *Teachers and Teaching: Theory and Practice*, Vol. 9, No. 3, 2003, pp.197–211

Supervision/feedback

Baron, W. and Strong, M., 'An analysis of mentoring conversations with beginning teachers: suggestions and responses', *Teaching and Teacher Education*, Vol. 20, No. 1, 2004, pp.47–57

Chalies, S., 'Interactions between pre-service and cooperating teachers and knowledge construction during post-lesson interviews', *Teaching and Teacher Education*, Vol. 20, No. 8, 2004, pp.765–81

Hawkey, K., 'Consultative supervision and mentor development: an initial exploration and case study', *Teachers and Teaching: Theory and Practice*, Vol. 4, No. 2, 1998, pp.331–48

John, P.D., 'Winning and losing: a case of university tutor-student teacher interaction during a school-based practicum', *Mentoring and tutoring*, Vol. 9, No. 2, 2001, pp.153–68

Sosik, J.J. and Godshalk, V.M., 'Examining gender similarity and mentor's supervisory status in mentoring relationships', *Mentoring and tutoring*, Vol. 13, No. 1, 2005, pp.39–52

Mentor/coach – role and development

Elliott, B. and Calderhead, J., 'Mentoring for teacher development: possibilities and caveats', in McIntyre, D., Hagger, H. and Wilkin, M. (eds), *Mentoring: Perspectives on School-Based Teacher Education*, London: Kogan Page, 1993, pp.54–67

Francis Lopez-Real, F. and Kwan, T., 'Mentors' perceptions of their own professional development during mentoring', *Journal of Education for Teaching*, Vol. 31, No. 1, 2005, pp.15–24

Franke, A. and Dahlgren, L.O., 'Conceptions of mentoring: an empirical study of conceptions of mentoring during the school-based teacher education', *Teaching and Teacher Education*, Vol. 12, No. 6, 1996, pp.627–41

Glover, D., Gough, G. and Johnson, M. with Taylor, M., 'Towards a taxonomy of mentoring', *Mentoring and tutoring*, Vol. 2, No. 2, 1994, pp.25–39

Harvard, G. and Dunne, R., 'The role of the mentor in developing teacher competence', *Westminster Studies in Education*, Vol. 15, No. 1, 1992, pp.33–44

Hobson, A.J., 'Student teachers' perceptions of mentoring in initial teacher training (ITT)', *Mentoring and tutoring*, Vol. 10, No. 1, 2002, pp.5–20

Millwater, J. and Yarrow, A., 'The mentoring mindset: a constructivist perspective?', *Mentoring and tutoring*, Vol. 5, No. 1, 1997, pp.14–24

Orland-Barak, L., 'What's in a case?: what mentors' cases reveal about the practice of mentoring', *Journal of Curriculum Studies*, Vol. 34, No. 4, 2002, pp.451–68

Roberts, A., 'Mentoring revisited: a phenomenological reading of the literature', *Mentoring and tutoring*, Vol. 8, No. 2, 2000, pp.145–70

Saunders, S., Pettinger, K. and Tomlinson, P., 'Prospective mentors' views on partnership in secondary teacher training', *British Educational Research Journal*, Vol. 21, No. 2, 1995, pp.199–218

NQTs/induction

Bleach, K., *The Induction and Mentoring of Newly Qualified Teachers: A New Deal for Teachers*, London: David Fulton, 1999

Bubb, S., Heilbronn, R., Jones, C., Totterdell, M. and Bailey, M., *Improving*

Induction: A Guide for Schools, London: Routledge Falmer, 2002

Cross, R., 'The role of the mentor in utilising the support system for the Newly Qualified Teacher', *School Organisation*, Vol. 15, No. 1, 1995, pp.35–42

Fletcher, S. and Barrett, A., 'Developing effective beginning teachers through mentor-based induction', *Mentoring and tutoring*, Vol. 12, No. 3, 2004, pp.321–33

Hayes, D., *The Handbook for Newly Qualified Teachers*, London: David Fulton, 2000

Heaney, S., 'Experience of induction in one Local Education Authority', *Mentoring and tutoring*, Vol. 9, No. 3, 2001, pp.241–54

Kelley, L.M., 'Why Induction Matters', *Journal of Teacher Education*, Vol. 55, No. 5, 2004, pp.438–48

Kenward, H., *An Induction Manual for Newly Qualified and Returning Teachers*, London: David Fulton, 2001

Rippon, J. and Martin, M., 'Supporting Induction: relationships count', *Mentoring and tutoring*, Vol. 11, No. 2, 2003, pp.195–210

Simco, N. and Carroll, C., *Succeeding as an Induction Tutor, Effective Support for NQTs*, Exeter: Learning Matters, 2001

Tickle, L., *Teacher Induction: The Way Ahead*, Buckingham: OUP, 2000

TTA, *The Role of the Induction Tutor: Principles and Guidance*, London: TTA, 2001

TTA, *Into Induction: An Introduction for Trainee Teachers to the Induction Period for Newly Qualified Teachers*, London: TTA, 2001

Williams, A.E. and Prestage, S., 'The Induction tutor: mentor manager or both?' *Mentoring and tutoring*, Vol. 10, No. 1, 2002, pp.35–46

Mentoring mid-career teachers

Fabian, H. and Simpson, A., 'Mentoring the experienced teacher', *Mentoring and tutoring*, Vol. 10, No. 2, 2002, pp.117–25

Pyatt, G., 'Cross-school mentoring: training and implementing a peer mentoring strategy', *Mentoring and tutoring*, Vol. 10, No. 2, 2002, pp.171–7

Shank, M.J., 'Mentoring among high school teachers: a dynamic and reciprocal group process', *Mentoring and tutoring*, Vol. 13, No. 1, 2005, pp.73–82

Bibliography

Ackley, B. and Gall, M.D., 'Skills, strategies and outcomes of successful mentor teachers', paper presented at the meeting of the American Educational Research Association, San Francisco, (ERIC Document Reproduction Service No. ED 346 046), 1992

Capel, S., 'Responsibilities of subject mentors, professional mentors and link tutors in secondary physical education initial teacher training', *Mentoring and tutoring*, Vol. 11, No. 2, August 2003

Carr, W. and Kemmis, S., *Becoming critical: educational knowledge and action research*, London: Falmer Press, 1986

Cole, M. and Stuart, J.S., '"Do you ride on elephants?" and "Never tell them you are German": the experiences of British Asian and black, and overseas student teachers in SE England', *British Educational Research Association*, Vol. 31, No. 3, June 2005

Department for Education (DFE), *Initial Teacher Training (secondary phase)*, Circular 9/92, London: DfE, 1992

Edwards, A., 'Possible futures for initial teacher education in the primary phase', in Hudson, A. and Lambert, D. (eds), *Exploring Futures for Initial Teacher Education: changing key for changing times*, London: Bedford Way Papers, 1998

Elliott, J. (ed.), *Reconstructing Teacher Education*, London: Falmer Press, 1993

Elliott, B. and Calderhead, J., 'Mentoring for Teacher Development: possibilities and caveats', in McIntyre, D., Hagger, H. and Wilkin, M. (eds), *Mentoring Perspectives on School-Based Teacher Education*, London: Kogan Page, 1993, pp.54–67

Errington, E. (ed.), *Developing scenario-based learning: Practical Insights for Tertiary Educators*, New Zealand: Dunmore Press Ltd, 2003

Evans, L., Abbott, R., Goodyear, R. and Pritchard, A., 'Is there a role for Higher Education in initial teacher training? A consideration of some of the main issues in the current debate', *Higher Education Quarterly*, Vol. 50, No. 2, pp.138–55, in Hobson, A.J., 'Student Teachers' Perceptions of School-based Mentoring in Initial Teacher Training (ITT)', *Mentoring and tutoring*, Vol. 10, No.1, 2002

Fish, D., *Quality Mentoring for Trainee Teachers: A Principled Approach to Practice*, London: David Fulton, 1995

Gilles, C. and Wilson, J., 'Receiving as well as giving: Mentors' perceptions of their professional development in one teacher induction programme', *Mentoring and tutoring*, Vol. 12, No.1, April 2004

Hobson, A.J., 'Student Teachers' Perceptions of School-based Mentoring in Initial Teacher Training (ITT)', *Mentoring and tutoring*, Vol.10, No.1, 2002

Johnson-Bailey, J. and Cervero, R.M., 'Mentoring in black and white: the intricacies of cross-cultural mentoring', *Mentoring and tutoring*, Vol.12, No. 1, April 2004

Lave, J. and Wenger, E., *Situated Learning: legitimate peripheral participation*, Cambridge: Cambridge University Press, 1991

Malderez, A., 'New ELT professionals', *English Teaching Professional*, 19, pp.57–8, 2001, in Hobson, A.J., 'Student Teachers' Perceptions of School-based Mentoring in Initial teacher Training (ITT)', *Mentoring and tutoring*, Vol.10, No.1, 2002

Maynard, M., 'The limits of mentoring: the contribution of the HE tutor to primary trainee-teachers' school-based learning', in Furlong, J. and Smith, R. (eds), *The Role of Higher Education in Initial Teacher Training*, London: Kogan Page, 1996

Maynard, T. and Furlong, J., 'Learning to Teach and Models of Mentoring', in McIntyre, D., Hagger, H. and Wilkin, M. (eds), *Mentoring Perspectives on School-based Teacher Education*, London: Kogan Page, 1993, pp.69–85

McIntyre, D., 'A research agenda for initial teacher education', in *Teacher Education Research in a New Context: The Oxford Internship Scheme*, London: Paul Chapman, 1997, pp.1–15

Mee-Lee, L. and Bush, T., 'Trainee mentoring in HE: Hong Kong Baptist University', *Mentoring and tutoring*, Vol. 11, No. 3, December 2003

Race Relations Amendment Act (2000) available online at: <http://www.hmso.gov.uk/acts/acts2000/20000034.htm>

Rogoff, B., 'Observing sociocultural activity on three planes: participatory appropriation, guided participation, apprenticeship', in Wertsch, J.W., Alvarez, A. and Del Rio, P. (eds), *Sociocultural studies of Mind*, Cambridge:

Cambridge University Press, 1995, pp.139–64

Saunders, S., Pettinger, K. and Tomlinson, P., 'Prospective Mentors' views on partnership in secondary teacher training', *British Educational Research Journal*, Vol. 21, No.2, 1995, pp.199–218

Schon, D., *The Reflective Practitioner*, New York: Basic Books, 1983

Sivan, A. and Chan, D.W.K., 'Supervised Teaching Practice as a Partnership Process: novice and experienced student-teachers' perceptions', *Mentoring and tutoring*, Vol. 11, No. 2, August 2003

Stevens, R.J., *Teaching in American Schools*, Columbus, OH: Merrill, 1999

Stewart, T.M., 'Essential slices of reality: Constructing problem-based scenarios that work', in Errington, E. (ed.), *Developing scenario-based learning: Practical Insights for Tertiary Educators*, New Zealand: Dunmore Press Ltd, 2003

Tomlinson, P.D., Donnelly, J.F., Roper, T., Sugden, D.A. , Welford, A.G. and Whitelaw, S.A., *Learning Class Management: Still the hardest lesson?*, University of Leeds, School of Education, 1996

Von Glaserfeld, E., 'Introduction: aspects of constructivism', in Fosnot, C.T. (ed.), *Constructivism: theory, perspectives and practice*, New York: Teachers College Press, 1996

Vygotsky, L.S., *Thought and Language* (ed. Kouzulin, A.), Massachusetts: MIT Press, 1987

Yeomans, R. and Sampson, J., *Mentoring in the Primary School*, London: Falmer Press, 1994

Zachary, L.J., *The Mentor's guide*, San Francisco, CA: Jossey-Bass, 2000

Havering Sixth Form College Library

6520598